An American Childhood

David Contosta
Philip Hazelton

Illustrations by Julia Olszewski

Author's Note

An American Childhood was born some years ago when my first cousin Philip Hazelton and I, with our respective broods, converged on the old hometown to celebrate Thanksgiving at his parents' home, where our large extended family had assembled for this annual feast for as long as anyone could remember. After dinner that afternoon—and Thanksgiving dinners like Sunday dinners were always served at around one o'clock—Phil and I fell into talking about our childhoods.

   Before I went back to my history "professing business" in Philadelphia (as Phil always teased me), and he returned to his "preaching business" at his current Presbyterian church (as I invariably teased him), we agreed to continue sharing stories over email. Eventually, the idea emerged that we would organize the stories into chapters to share with the rest of the family, and later aim them at a larger audience who would enjoy them, too.

We decided not to name the town where we had grown up, thinking that our childhood might stand for "every town" and resonate with readers in other parts of the country. Still, there are some unintentional clues in the writing, which if someone wants to follow them carefully, they can pull back the curtain. And, of course, anyone who has known Phil or me would recognize the place immediately.

Sadly, Phil is no longer with us, but his imagination, his humor, and his amazing storytelling skills live on in this book. I am therefore very pleased that our immensely talented young illustrator Julia Olszewski has brought our stories to life in ways that Phil, a talented illustrator in his own right, would have very much appreciated. I am also indebted to the editorial and design assistance of Brent Spears whose enthusiasm for this memoir has kept the project alive. Additional thanks are due to Esther Reisberg and A. E. Williams.

David Contosta

January 2022

1. Hometown Ways

Our town had known a headier past. It thrived in the early nineteenth century at the intersection of two important wagon roads; then in the 1830s, it became a booming canal town. Eager men and women settled in, there to make good livings and rear large families. A few residents gained national reputations as U.S. Senators, cabinet secretaries, and presidential hopefuls. One was a celebrated Civil War general. However, the bonanza fizzled when the trunk line railroads went 15 miles or so to the north. It was then that the town slipped into the modest but steady growth we knew as kids.

We didn't need anyone to point out that our community was exactly 30 miles from the state capital, since the highway signs downtown announced this fact in bold black letters every two or three blocks. These 30 miles were a unit of distance that we would reference over and over, after we had moved away from home and tried to explain to new friends and neighbors where we had grown up: "About 30 miles from the state capital," we still say, sure that they have never heard of our town. These 30 miles were also a handy measuring rod for our parents to describe a moderately long drive: "That's like a trip to the State House," they'd say.

Less obvious was the fact that the town lay about a dozen miles south of old U.S. Route 40, a ribbon of highway, now largely replaced by Interstate 70, which linguists and historians alike have come to see as something of a fuzzy boundary between North and South, at least in cultural attitudes. Although we lived just a few miles south of this divide, our town was really at a transition point between the two sections, snuggling just below the first foothills of the Appalachian chain in a wide valley surrounded by a rim of low hills. Further south and east of town spread a rugged landscape, through which we drove with the family, and sometimes hiked under brilliant fall colors. This was a poor land of played-out mines and poisoned streams, a blighted and smoky place where many impoverished families lived. Every house seemed to come with a battered jalopy propped up on blocks in the front yard and a skinny old dog lazing under the trees. We heard stories of moonshine stills back in the woods and of fights with federal "revenuers," which may have been more myth than reality.

A decade later Michael Harrington's book, *The Other America*, revealed that approximately one-fourth of the American people lived in a culture of poverty and that a significant portion of them inhabited areas like those just below our town. Harrington's book helped to stir a national conversation that led to the launch of President Lyndon Johnson's War on Poverty in 1964. Of course, Johnson and his Democratic Party were not especially popular among middle-class folks in our part of the world. People were poor, we had heard adults say again and again, because they were innately lazy, and government handouts would only make them lazier. This was a crude, but popular version of what scholars had long called social Darwinism.

We could hardly fail to see the difference between the deprivation south of town, and the miles of gently rolling agricultural fields just to the north. Up there, farm kids raised prize-winning cattle and hogs for the 4-H, and many went off to college and satisfying careers. The choice between well-tended farms or rickety mountain shacks was a matter of which way our dads pointed the family car on a Sunday afternoon. But the idea that geography could go a long way to explain the differences between prosperous farmers and poor families down in the hills—rather than varying degrees of the work ethic—didn't seem to occur to most adults we knew.

The town itself was unlike either of these familiar places just beyond municipal boundaries. During those prosperous postwar years, it supported bustling industries and a flourishing commercial district, along with all the doctors, lawyers, teachers, and service workers essential to health and well-being.

Despite the overall prosperity, we sensed that there were genuine social and economic divisions within the community. One of the best places to see these differences was downtown on a Saturday afternoon, in this era before malls and shopping centers. "Downtown" was

strung out along two or three blocks of Main Street, with
another set of stores on the two cross streets. Built mainly
of red brick, the commercial buildings were dressed up in
several styles, from late Federal and Mansard to grandiose
Roman Revival banks. A few were plain office buildings
put up in the teens and twenties of the twentieth century.
Some of the buildings had false second stories (like those

in wild-west towns that we saw in the movies) and tried to look more important than they were.

On the corner of Main and Broad streets, there was a small square laid out by the town fathers a century and a half before. In it were trees, lawns, and dark green metal park benches. Populating these seats on summer afternoons were tobacco-spitting old men who did not suffer children gladly. We sometimes wondered if we would end up there in another seventy years, with nothing to do but pass the days talking and spitting on the same benches, whose layers of chipped paint made them look as worn as the old fellows who occupied them day after day.

We could escape from these visions of crackled old age to the ornate Victorian fountain that sat on the opposite corner of the square. Put up in the regime of Benjamin Harrison, it had been a trophy of civic pride for decades, proof that our townspeople had as much eye for beauty as people in the big city. To be honest, this fancy fountain seemed a little out of place in the middle of our otherwise plain downtown, since its fat, naked babies and a half-dressed maiden pouring water from a jar atop the fountain seemed suspiciously foreign and a little naughty.

Another corner of the square displayed cannons from several wars. We knew they were there to honor local sons who had gone off to fight for their country and had never returned, yet it seemed strange that we memorialized these unlucky young men with the sorts of weapons that had sent them to their early graves.

It was to these downtown streets that people came from everywhere in town, and the surrounding county, to shop on Saturday afternoons. Even as kids, we could tell exactly "who was who". Middle-class matrons wore one of their better dresses, complete with white gloves and hat. Women from farms, we thought (probably unfairly), were a bit over-weight with thick ankles. Their dresses were long, shapeless affairs, polka-dotted or covered with little swirly designs. They wore old-fashioned hats and black-laced shoes with wide heels, and no gloves. It seemed that women from down in the hills came to town with pallid skin, sunken eyes, and boney features. Half a century later, the bustle and hustle of downtown is a mere memory, as shopping centers and big box retail stores on the outskirts of town undermined and then obliterated the old commercial zone.

Our sense of social class was thus crudely visual and lacked the analysis of the systematic scholar. Without attempting such a study, a backward glance at the social scene might go something like this: at the heart of our productive population were several thousand workers, many of whom labored for the local glass company. It operated two plants in town, in addition to a large research facility and the company's corporate headquarters. The firm's most important product was a cheap line of tableware, which sold well in this period before massive imports. A smaller glass operation, several iron foundries, machine shops, shoe factories, and a modest electronics industry rounded out the list of major employers. The men and women who toiled their lives away in these hot and dirty places earned respect for their regular, workaday ways, but they were not among the movers and shakers in town.

Above the factory workers in the social pecking order (and at the lower rungs of the middle class) were those employed in such tasks as store clerks, bank tellers, and secretaries, who probably made less money than the factory workers, but who prided themselves on wearing better clothes and working in clean, well-lighted rooms.

Confusing for us kids were outward appearances that caused us to think they were much more influential than they were, since they looked so official sitting at their typewriters or behind department store counters and bank teller cages.

A rank or two above were the shop owners, factory managers, and teachers, who occupied the very middle of our middle class. Teachers enjoyed this distinction more because of their degrees—and from the general esteem in which everyone held them—than because of the meager salaries they received. Above this group, at the top of our middle class, were lawyers, business executives, and especially the doctors.

In those days, all our doctors were men, who basked in an exalted status that had no equal among other professionals. Local wags insisted, "M.D." meant "minor deity." We lesser mortals envied their substantial incomes and their fancy diplomas, which represented a vast body of knowledge that was unfathomable to the average citizen. Only later did we find out that the medical man's understanding of the wider world could be somewhat narrow.

We also noticed that social climbers liked to drop the names of alleged doctor friends. Some adults hung on every word from the family healer, including his political and social opinions. Politically, some of our doctors belonged to the far right, several of them organizing a local chapter of the John Birch Society. And virtually all of them denounced the idea of national health insurance as "socialized medicine." If in an earlier generation, mothers had wanted their sons to be ministers, priests, or foreign missionaries (and all prestigious career desires were male oriented in our childhood), by the 1950s that dream had been replaced by a life in medicine. Perhaps this was because doctors were not quite as rich or mysterious as descendants of one of the old families in town. In that sense, doctors were much more accessible than the local aristocrats were, and at least in theory were part of a merit system that did not depend entirely on inherited wealth or prestige.

At the very top of our local society were two dozen or so heirs of the "old families," most of them living in large antebellum houses—impressive Federal and Greek Revival dwellings—that lined several deeply shaded streets on the hill just north of downtown. We knew these people only by their family names, the same names that graced our parks and streets. Since we never saw them, we assumed they might just as easily be in Palm Beach than at home. When we tried to picture them, we imagined tweedy women with straight, rich hair and long noses, whose husbands could tell a polo pony from a croquet ball, and who spoke, we imagined, with some sort of clipped East Coast accent. We later discovered that there was more fantasy than truth to this stereotype, one that was probably fueled by our desire to believe such exalted creatures lived among us. Yet a few of them had traveled in Europe, had attended Ivy League colleges, and had sent their children to private boarding schools in the East. Some really did go to Chicago or New York to buy clothes.

At the opposite end of our pecking order were a dozen or so Black families who had lived in town for decades. Most of us referred to them as "negroes" or "colored people," but it was all too common to overhear less enlightened adults call them by the "n" word, either as a matter of course or in the process of telling a racist joke or making a racial slur. Rumor had it that local Blacks had policed themselves for years by discouraging "undesirable" members of their race, generally thought to originate from anywhere outside of town, from moving in and "causing trouble." One of us later discovered through an interview with an elderly black resident that this was, in fact, no rumor.

We knew these Black citizens held the most menial jobs such as sweeping out stores at night, working as domestic servants, or operating a shoeshine stand downtown. Our schools did not practice segregation, but the number of black students was small. During our parents' childhoods, we heard that Blacks could go to the municipal swimming pool just once a week—the day before they changed the water (which was also later confirmed in an interview). We learned many years later that this sort of segregation on separate days at swimming pools was common in many communities, unless Blacks were banned altogether.

Looking back, we recognize other examples of racial inequality. For instance, we often heard adults say, "The colored people are all right as long as they stay in their place" or, "The colored just have to be patient and earn their rights." Residents could also be overheard, asking rhetorically, "Don't you just thank God you weren't born colored?" In the same breath, they were likely to add, "If I was colored, I'd get my kids into sports or show business—it's the only way out."

Where our very few Black classmates went for dates was something that never bothered us. The very notion of interracial dating was abhorrent to everyone we knew, and any transgression of this boundary would have marked any white individual involved in such a relationship as a pariah for life, and have subjected the Black partner, if he were male, to the real possibility of violence. Nor were we concerned that our Black classmates would have had to accept some sort of menial job after graduation—either that or leave town in hopes of finding a better position in the big city. Such feelings toward African Americans in our town represented one of the most flagrant hypocrisies of our place and time. For it was a blatant contradiction between what we were told on patriotic holidays and many other occasions (at home, as well as at school and church) about the unique freedom and equality of America—and our failure to practice these ideals in everyday life. It was only later during the civil rights movement of the 1960s that we truly realized the contradiction and marveled at our willingness to accept it during those growing-up years.

There was no possibility that the one daily newspaper in town would question prevailing social arrangements. Although it reported the rare sensational crime, most of the stories were of the booster variety. There was a "society page" that appeared once a week, which covered such things as bridge clubs, family reunions, golf outings, wedding engagements and anniversaries, and the vacations of more well-to-do families. There was also a weekly column of reminiscences. These recounted pleasant, local happenings that had taken place ten, twenty, thirty, or forty "years ago." Each fall, the paper listed the names of farmers in the surrounding countryside who had made it into the "100-Acre Corn Club"—that is, consisting of farmers whose efforts had yielded a hundred or more bushels of corn per acre. There were lists, too, of births and deaths and of persons admitted to the local hospital (in those days before HIPPA privacy laws). However, the newspaper never carried critical stories about the main industry in town, a large glass-making concern, since the company owned a majority interest in the paper. Nor was there any real investigative journalism or crusades against political corruption or pressing social problems.

As to the white majority in town, most were native-born and of northern European backgrounds, as we could guess (at least when we were older) from reading the graves markers in the local cemeteries. The most widely represented group were of German ancestry, with stone after stone announcing the final resting place of a Miller (originally Mueller), a Graf, a Schneider, or numerous variations on the suffix -burg or -man(n). This should not have surprised us in a community that counted so many Pennsylvania Germans (also known as Pennsylvania

Dutch) families among its pioneer generation and continued to receive immigrants directly from Germany throughout the nineteenth century.

The descendants of southern mountain English and Scotch-Irish settlers also made their claims in the cemetery, as did old-stock Americans from New England and the Middle Atlantic states. Italians and eastern Europeans, on the other hand, were almost as rare as Martians, while Asians and Latinos were never even imagined.

This is not to say that adults lacked curiosity about family connections among townspeople. One of our mothers' favorite pastimes was to sit with friends or relatives in endless discussions about who was related to whom, who had married whom, or when the individual under discussion had graduated from the local high school: "Oh, she was a Schaefer before she got married and graduated with me in '37," one of our mothers began. To that an aunt replied, "No, I think she was a Frazier and graduated with our brother back in '31." The talk continued until the guessing played itself out and some other topic replaced it. Although the same names surfaced every year or so, our mothers never came up with any firm answers. Sometimes they dug out an old high school yearbook to prove a point. Such appeals were rare, since the real and perhaps unrecognized purpose of this game was not to come up with exact information, but to reaffirm a sense of belonging to a web of local friends and acquaintances.

In contrast, we cast men and women from beyond our immediate area into the role of "outsider". Most of us were glad we didn't live down in the hills—or up in the state capital, which we saw as a big, dirty city with all sorts of undesirable people. However, our most potent image of the big city was New York.

Although New York had the reputation among us of a modern Sodom and Gomorrah—a cold, wicked, and unfeeling city—it also stood for urban excitement and rich living. We experienced its glamour vicariously in countless movies and knew from a very early age that New York was the center of fashion, high finance, and savior faire (even if we didn't know that word). New York was also home to the Yankees, who in those days, automatically won the World Series, except when the Dodgers or the Giants—also then from New York—claimed the prize. We also knew it as the Gotham of Batman, the Metropolis of Superman, and the home of King Kong and other superior beings.

Those folks from our town who went off to New York on business trips—or, more impressively, on shopping expeditions—took on an aura of sophistication that could not have been topped by their rocketing off to Jupiter for a day. After a visit to the metropolis, the travelers came back feeling a little superior to the rest of us rustics, often with the annoying habit of mentioning the trip for months to come.

Among these bold adventurers was a favorite uncle who took occasional trips to New York on business, or for a Shriner's convention, forays that gave him the mystique of a man of the world. Once, he came home with a small, plastic half-toilet mounted on a wooden plaque. Under it was an inscription that read "For my half-assed friends." This treasure hung on his bathroom wall for years and may still be there. We sensed that our mothers disapproved of it, but they never said anything, at least to us. Even this cheap and slightly naughty souvenir did not alter our opinion of its owner's worldliness, for if the object came from New York, we concluded that it had to be the latest in creativity.

New York held such a mystique that we liked to remind ourselves that the highway which became our Main

Street was also the road that led to Gotham. The road wound all the way to the Empire State Building, causing us to examine passing cars and trucks to see if they had New York license plates. Still, we never tired of repeating the old cliché, as if it were the wisdom of the Bible, "New York is a nice place to visit, but you wouldn't want to live there."

This smug phrase not only reflected our general contentment with the hometown, but it also betrayed our ambivalence about New York and the East Coast in general. We admired the East as the scene of our nation's early history, and for the standards it set in culture and fashions. We also resented, in this era when California's great impact was just beginning to be felt, that Easterners had far too much influence over the rest of the country. We thought New York, especially, had no right to dictate clothing styles to the rest of us, or to dominate the airwaves and financial markets. In the early days of television, we noticed that virtually every network program was set in New York—whether live or on film. Even the jokes on television were about life in New York, referring to such exotic things as subways, automats, and doormen, which made little sense to us.

The suspicion that Easterners thought they were somehow superior rankled us, and when people moved to town from the East, usually as the result of a transfer to one of our industries, they were a bit suspect until we learned that they were not much different from the rest of us. Years later, when Vice President Spiro Agnew tore into the New York-dominated news media and the "Eastern Establishment," he knowingly touched that old sore spot for many in our town. Indifference to New York's near bankruptcy in the mid-1970s was another manifestation of that old mixture of envy and inferiority.

We later discovered that this sense of "we" and "they," also known as tribalism, unfortunately plays out in every community in the country—and, no doubt, around the world. While we looked down on the hill people or thanked God that we didn't live in some large city, we also feared that people from other parts of the state sneered at us. Our big city cousins made fun of our small-town ways and bragged about their supposedly more sophisticated lives. We also suspected that big city people driving through town might be laughing at us.

Whatever we thought about other peoples' opinions, we pointed with pride to all evidence of local importance as a way of banishing self-doubt. Besides bragging about our famous residents from the past, we took heart from the fact that Malcolm Forbes had begun his publishing career in town during the late 1930s with a small daily, and later a weekly, newspaper. Just after World War II, he featured us in his new *Forbes* magazine as a prosperous, small manufacturing town.

However, the biggest event of the postwar era was when Hollywood showed up to film a portion of the horse story, *The Green Grass of Wyoming*, in our local fairgrounds. We were thrilled to know, that living in our very midst for a few weeks, were such stars as Burl Ives, Charles Coburn, Lloyd Nolan, Peggy Cummins, and various lesser lights. It didn't matter one whit to us that the movie, a story about a young man's belief in his horse, was not a critical success. A "grand opening" took place at our largest movie house. On the street just outside the Palace Theater, we read the words "THE GREEN GRASS OF WYOMING" emblazoned in huge green letters. Once inside, we scanned the crowd scenes, hoping for a glimpse of local bit players or for our own small faces in the grandstand. The excitement of that whole event lifted us out of our everyday lives and left a special glow that lasted for years. Much later, parts of another movie called *Brubaker*, starring Robert Redford, were filmed locally. But it did not cast the same spell as *the Green Grass of Wyoming*, made just before television had robbed the movies of their old magic.

Postwar politics did create some mild divisions. It did not take us long to realize that the Republican Party in our town was synonymous with respectability. Because most members of our family were Republicans, we accepted the party line. Even in our childhood, we heard the old slurs against the Democrats, such as, "Not every Democrat's a horse thief, but every horse thief's a Democrat." We associated the Democratic Party with political hacks, union men, unassimilated immigrants, welfare cheats, and, hypocritically, with bigoted Southerners. Most of all, we believed that the Democrats stood for everything "we were not." The Republicans, in contrast, were the choice of decent, hard-working family men—of prosperous doctors, lawyers, wholesome businessmen, and everyone else who believed in basic American values.

We associated these qualities with the presidency of Dwight David Eisenhower, a man who personified everything about the respectable Republican leader. Ike seemed to be above politics, a smiling, strong, no-nonsense leader who preferred, whenever possible, to run the free world through genuine good will or a Dutch uncle talk with a stubborn congressman or discontented foreign ally. On the other hand, we heard our parents and other adults say that Democratic President Harry S. Truman was a tool of corrupt city machines and union rabble-rousers. It was years before we could admire Truman for his personal honesty, feisty character, and deep reading of world and national history. We were also shocked to learn years later that there were many Democrats besides Franklin Roosevelt (a mild anathema in our family)—men such as Francis Biddle and Averill Harriman—who came from wealthy, socially prominent families. Yet compared to the political polarization that would characterize the United States several decades later, voters in our town were often willing to "split tickets" and vote, especially in local elections, for candidates they thought would do the best job of dealing with local problems, especially if the candidate were a friend, neighbor, or former classmate. It was also not unheard of for someone to cross party lines in voting for president.

Still, there were plenty of politicians in our youth who gained and held onto power by inflaming the Cold War. This was especially true of Republicans who were desperate to win back the White House after 20 years of Democratic rule. We, accordingly, heard local and national Republicans hammering away at Truman and his party for having lost China to the Communists. It did not seem to matter that China did not belong to us and was not "ours" to lose in the first place, and that there was nothing the United States could do, short of a massive, full-scale war, to alter events in China.

Some adults we knew suspected the motives of all foreign powers and maintained that the United States should not waste its time and money (foreign aid) on people who didn't understand or appreciate the "American way of life," or who simply wanted to mooch off our country. Of course, such isolationism was in obvious contradiction to the fervent demands, often uttered by the same individuals, to stand up against the Communists. In fact, isolationism and anti-Communism were two sides of the same coin: Communism was simply another alien doctrine that we had to keep out of the United States.

Meanwhile, we shouldn't spend our blood and treasure on corrupt and vicious countries around the world.

Such contradictions were lost on most of our elders and would have made little sense to us at the time. What we did experience were the physical, verbal, and psychological manifestations of anti-Communist concerns in our own town. One aspect of it was the fear of sneak attack from Communist aircrafts. The Ground Observer Corps (GOC), we understood, had been established to prevent such a catastrophe. We had a unit of this vigilant group in town, with a headquarters and watchtower on one of the hills just north of the corporation limits. Into this facility went volunteers, including our own parents and neighbors, who signed up for four-hour stretches. Armed with binoculars and a slide-window device that pictured the silhouettes of various aircraft, our dads (and sometimes moms) occasionally took us along with them to scan the skies for enemy planes. The main target of these Communist bombers, authorities said, was an airbase just outside our state capital. While our parents were gazing into the skies, we ran up and down the hill pretending to battle the Russians (officially the Soviets) or the Chinese.

We did not realize at the time that neither the Soviets nor the Chinese were close enough to launch air attacks against our part of the world, in that time before intercontinental ballistic missiles. It is not surprising that none of the Ground Observer volunteers sighted a single enemy aircraft. The volunteers who gave up their time for this futile task were not a pack of right-wing "crazies," but honest citizens who had been convinced by cynical politicians that the fear was real, and that the enemy was at our gates.

Far more serious was the way in which the great Red Scare of the postwar years infected our youthful lives with fear and suspicion. Outspoken members of the community, for example, were suspect until proven otherwise. When a new minister, from the big city, proposed in a Sunday sermon that we should be more open to the emerging black Civil Rights Movement, we saw the knowing looks around the congregation that seemed to say, "We'd better watch him; he just might be a little pink." Worse, we carried around the frightening image of ruthless Soviet invaders, doubtlessly inspired by World War II movies that showed strutting, brutal soldiers marching down the street of some European town as local citizens huddled in silent fear along curbs and roadsides. Our localization of world events, so that all great matters became comprehensible in the context of our town, was thus driven by fear: "Someday, one day," we thought, "I hope it never happens--They'll *come for us* with their great bombers and tanks and pale-eyed soldiers."

It was adults, of course, who transferred these fears to us. One day while we cousins were delivering newspapers, an elderly woman called from her porch stoop, "How old are you boys?"

"Twelve and eight," we said.

"Boys," she croaked, "You ain't gonna live to be 18. Them Rooshians is gona get ya! Don't think they're not'a flyun over here right now and watchun yooo?"

These ravings of an elderly neighbor were reinforced by fears of internal subversion and rot. More hysterical adults said that postwar prosperity had made us soft and weak, unable to see the traitors in our midst, and unprepared to defend ourselves against enemies at home or abroad. Our parents' generation, they added, had been toughened by the Great Depression and were better prepared to face the Nazis and Japanese than we would ever be to take on the Communists. Better-read citizens wondered aloud if the United States was not like the Roman Empire in its first stages of decline. They failed to remember that Americans in the 1930s had been woefully unprepared for war and very reluctant to stand up to international tyrannies until the "sneak attack" at Pearl Harbor gave the United States no choice but to enter the war. Or maybe these comparisons between levels of preparedness, however false, were our elders' ways of trying to keep us from repeating their own mistakes.

For the more historically minded members of our parents' generation the biggest international mistake of their early adulthood had been British Prime Minister Neville Chamberlain's disastrous attempt to appease Adolph Hitler at Munich. As one of our history teachers put it, "Pfffth, Munich! That's a word you spit out!" For him and for many adults who had lived through World War II, the lesson of Munich was clear. Our enemies would take even the sincerest efforts at compromise as a dangerous sign of weakness, and the lesson for us was evident: it meant an uncompromising stand by the free world against the Soviet Union, China, and their allies. Attempts to negotiate even the most mutually beneficial agreements were thus foolish. Such thinking often cast a pall over our youth and prolonged the Cold War for many years.

It was in such an atmosphere of fear and uncertainty that another youthful impression of danger came our way one warm summer afternoon as the local National Guard unit returned home from a two-week encampment, in full uniform and driving olive-green trucks. Watching the troops file by, we overheard several adults say, "Too bad. Nice young men. I hate to think of what God-forsaken place they'll be in next year!"

We should have been reassured that our country was the mightiest nation the world had ever known—at the pinnacle of its power and prestige. We should have also taken heart (and maybe even some pity) in the knowledge that the Soviet Union was still suffering from the Nazi onslaught only a decade or so before. Under the circumstances, the chances of a Soviet invasion of the United States in the 1950s were nil, even supposing that the Kremlin had real designs on the American nation. Adults never pointed out these facts to us, probably not knowing themselves. Hence, our own exaggerated fears of Communism were so powerful that being "the leader of the free world" only convinced us that we might have to die in the last great battle against the Communist devil. A decade later, we saw this whole fabric of fear and anxiety crumble, even as bankrupt leaders like Lyndon Johnson continued to parrot this old line of fear and paranoia, believing that if they evoked the same tired imagery of Communists with their planes and jackboots, we would scramble into our watchtowers again. As we were to discover, this obsession with Communism would become imbedded in our churches and schools.

It may be that the anti-Communist scare found fertile soil in our town, and in America as a whole, because we were more than ready to believe in dark conspiracies, or at least eager to believe that nothing was simple and on the surface. More than once, we heard adults talk about how the Mafia was supposedly in control of our small community, and that they "had the police chief in their pocket" as they carried on (in truth, non-existent) gambling and prostitution rackets.

A noted source of such dark rumors was a downtown sporting goods store, a popular hangout for men and boys, operated by a longtime resident, Bud Heffernan. His place always looked cluttered and outdated, with its false tin ceiling molded into rows of square indentions and displaying a Victorian floral design in the middle of each one. On the walls, we saw stuffed fish, deer antlers, and other long-ago hunting trophies; and on racks, there were the hunting and sports magazines, along with *Esquire*, *Playboy*, and other familiar publications of the day. Behind the counter, we eyed the racks of shiny new rifles and shot guns, along with boxes of shells with their red, green, or

copper-colored casings. In the aisles, we surveyed the shelves of hunting boots and jackets, fishing tackle, and cardboard cartons of gym suits and other sports gear, including an array of athletic supports, which he stocked at the request of the local high school. Even if we had gone in blindfolded, the smells of Bud's store were unmistakable—

a combination of heavy tobacco smoke, gun-cleaning oil, and new football jerseys.

We never spent more than a few minutes in Bud's place without hearing some retail businessman unleash a tale of local conspiracy. According to him, a manufacturer in town "owned" several judges and politicians to do their bidding, while the firm held a veto power over any community project. He also whispered knowingly that the high school basketball coach was about to be fired because certain local men, whom he called "big shots," wanted him out. Then there was a mediocre athlete who got into the starting lineup because his father *had* something on the high school principal. The hangers on in the store nodded at these stories, knowing the "truth" of what was said.

These whispers and nods played to a desire for unseen drama. They also allowed individuals to claim a degree of victimhood or to provide them with simple explanations for confusing issues and complex problems. And any story that suggested that Communist agents were manipulating us through government, the school, or even the pulpit fitted in with a larger conspiratorial view of the world.

In a time of rumors and fears, we all took great pains to commemorate former battles against the nation's enemies. This remembrance was especially true on Memorial Day, in those days celebrated precisely on May 30 and not on the nearest Monday. The high point of the day was the big parade which passed by the end of our street around 9:30 in the morning.

Very faintly, at first, comes the flickering sound of the high school band playing a patriotic number of the John Philip Sousa type, or maybe the school's fight song. The teenaged musicians take breaks between tunes; only the sound of snare drums keeps up the pace, and, it seems, always just about the time they reach our perch on the corner. Our school colors, purple and gold, snap in the morning breeze, the musicians passing only inches in front of us, their faces as stiff as drumheads. It could easily be an army review, with its straight lines, pseudo military garb, and martial music.

Black police cars and shiny red fire trucks follow. Next, come a train of veteran groups and their auxiliaries: Gold Star Mothers riding on a flatbed truck; the American Legion in their blue jackets and peaked caps; the Veterans of Foreign Wars; and the Disabled American Veterans—

each flanked by gun and flag bearers. Most of the vets are World War II men, by now in their thirties. The survivors of the war in Korea are slightly younger but far fewer in number. Next come the World War I warriors, most of them more than able to march three to four decades after their crusade to make the world safe for democracy. There is even a Spanish-American War vet (who has been the county recorder forever, it seems) as grand marshal of the parade. He rides alone in a convertible up front. Only twenty or thirty years before, when our parents were children, an ancient Civil War campaigner had had the honor of leading the long file up the street.

Before us pass, silently and reverently, these men who have fought our twentieth-century wars, representing the soldiers, sailors, and aviators who did not live to share this bright May morning. We stand quietly and respectfully—our fathers curiously uneasy. Only later do we begin to understand the mixed emotions that survivors feel about surviving, or the horrors brought back to mind.

Additional units pass along: The National Guard, Daughters of Union Veterans, and the Red Cross; Boy Scouts, Girl Scouts, Campfire Girls, Brownies, Blue Birds, and a Civil Air Patrol contingent of high school boys. After a couple of minutes, they become a blaze of colors—brown and blue, khaki and red. Bobbing above are caps—overseas caps and scout caps, dull army green and polished metal helmets. There are badges, chevrons, epaulets, sashes, battle ribbons, flags, pennants, and rifles, congealed into a staccato blur of shuffling feet and barked commands. The next day our local newspaper runs a long description of the parade, concluding with a solemn warning: "This Memorial Day was one of renewed and fervent dedication at a time when the hydrogen bomb and other terrible weapons cast their grim shadows over the earth."

That is tomorrow, and we have yet to see the final units of the parade, which come abruptly and unceremoniously after the long lines of somber militarism. There are knots of little girls in their sequined costumes from the local dance and baton-twirling studios; a bevy of politicians and officeholders in borrowed convertibles that display realtors' signs and merchants' advertisements on the side panels; several church floats reminding us that "Jesus Saves." There are also seven or eight grizzled denizens of the County Home, formerly known as the "Poor House." They are men who today would be cast among the homeless, the destitute, or the mentally ill.

Every year they insist on marching and no one seems to object. One old man carries a faded flag and the rest follow the leader in their bib overalls and white sidewall haircuts. Maybe two or three are real veterans. One of them, overcome with the emotion of the day, breaks rank, refuses to march in line with the rest, and begins to make faces at the crowds standing along the curb. Another County Homer, who looks too young to be there, is seized by the attention he gets and secretly flashes his middle finger at a bunch of kids who are delighted at his bravado. We can tell the parade is finally over when several weaving rows of school children ride by on bicycles and tricycles, with red, white, and blue crepe paper woven through their wheel spokes, and colorful streamers flying from the handlebars.

Finally, the parade reaches the cemetery, named for another martial event involving a half-mythical maiden captured by the local Native Americans and then rescued by two brave pioneers. At the foot of a steep hill just inside the cemetery gates stands a small war memorial surrounded by flagpoles, veterans' insignia, and a granite stone marker decorated with the fading colors of the World War I Rainbow Division. A prominent Protestant minister, who has served as a chaplain in the European theater during

World War II, delivers the speech, filled with praises for the heroic dead. Like tomorrow's newspaper, it ends with a call for continued vigilance against the Communists, a new and much more dangerous enemy, he warns us, "Who want nothing more than to lay their blood-stained hands on what we Americans have fought so hard to preserve." A Boy Scout standing among the trees on the hillside blows taps, with a second bugler echoing him in the distance.

Such scenes helped to fix and define us. However, it was in our neighborhoods and families that we found a sharper focus for our young lives.

2. Neighborhood Ties

For lack of imagination, we knew the major residential zones in our town from the points on the compass: The North, South, and East Ends—and the lonelier West Side—as well as the small enclave just north of downtown where the old families lived on the hill. Putting this coveted enclave aside, we considered the East End to be the most desirable part of town. In the 1920s, upper-middle-class families had built red brick, Colonial Revival houses there. After the war, there was another flurry of building in this section, but by then the one-story,

ranch-style house was all the rage. So, it was the older East End of the 1920s that our parents admired.

The wrong side of the tracks was the South End, literally as well as figuratively. Although it had plenty of neat and tidy houses, what caught our attention most were the cheap bars, railroad sidings, junk yards, weed-infested lots, and dilapidated buildings. However, this depressed part of town occupied only a small fraction of local real estate.

The West Side was home to mostly workers in one of the glass factories. The place resembled a little world of its own, located as it was on bottomlands just west of the river, which, like the railroad tracks in the South End, represented a physical and emotional boundary. To get to the West Side, we had to walk or drive across one of three narrow bridges. The actual distance was short, and in a large city, it would be nothing. To us, however, a walk or drive of more than several blocks was both far and inconvenient.

"West Siders" also thought that it was a nuisance to make their way across town and so they had created their own small shopping district, complete with drugstores, dry cleaners, grocery stores, a post office, and a branch library.

There was also a Methodist Church on the West Side for the largely Protestant residents who found it trying, socially as well as logistically, to attend the big Methodist church across the river near downtown.

We sensed that the West Side was better off than the South End. The houses were newer and in better repair, put up during the first decades of the twentieth century. Most were single dwelling units, with a few double-decker rows and "twins" scattered here and there. Although such multiple units were and are very respectable in large eastern cities, we considered them substandard and felt sorry for families who had to live in them. Still, there was a real warmth and neighborhood spirit on the West Side. When we got older, we could walk down its streets on hot summer nights and see the men sitting on their front porches, holding a beer, and listening to a baseball game on the radio. We were a little afraid of the West Side kids, though, who had the reputation for being tough. "The West Side against the world," was their motto, and it was enough to scare most of us away until we were old enough to know better.

Far scarier were three entirely different locations, just on the edge of town or a few miles away. These were the Reform School, the Children's Home, and the Fresh Air Camps. Juvenile delinquents, in the vocabulary of the time, came to the reform school from various counties. (It was rumored that comedian Bob Hope had once been a resident.) The institution operated a lot like a strict military school. Sometimes on Sunday afternoons, we drove down with our parents to watch the boys in a dress parade, complete with a brass band. It was frightening to know that boys our own age could do something awful enough to be torn away from their families and put in a place like this. Adults only reinforced the nightmare when they half-jokingly warned us that we might end up there ourselves if we "didn't behave and mind our parents." A couple of teachers even said that every boy should go on a tour of the reform school at least once, as a warning against bad behavior.

The Children's Home was much pleasanter, but it, too, was a grim reminder that the world, including our own small corner of it, could be very hard on youngsters. Our hearts sank whenever we drove past the home in the family car, especially when parents said, "Don't you just thank God you don't have to live in the Children's Home?"

We had mixed feelings about the Fresh Air Camps, a collection of cabins up in the woods north of town that were built so disadvantaged kids could escape from hot streets for a week or two every summer. The camp was another reminder that we were much luckier than other kids in town were. Yet, we envied the good time they all seemed to have up in the woods without parents to pick at them.

Our own families lived on the North End of town. We knew, with some exceptions, that the houses were not as attractive as those in the East End, but as a place of modest comfort, it seemed preferable to either the South End or the West Side. Unfortunately, this belief caused us to look down on other sections of town, while we sometimes envied the supposedly luckier kids in what we thought were better neighborhoods. However, we comforted ourselves by saying that those kids were a bunch of snobs who wouldn't be much fun to play with anyway. Just as the town defined itself by comparison with other communities in the state and nation, we identified our neighborhoods by their alleged rankings in the local pecking order. In fact, our neat division of the town into the North, South, and East ends, and the West side could not have stood up to any close examination, since we later came to know that there were many subsections in each of them, both real and imagined.

When we were very young, our neighborhood extended no further than our own house and those just around it. Later it grew to include the whole block, and, still later, the two or three streets next to ours. Yet kids who lived four or five blocks away seemed part of a different world. Our parents emphasized this feeling by referring to more distant families as "the Fair Avenue crowd"—or as "those folks over on Union Street." These vague categories were even more tangible because architectural styles might change every block or two. Since the town had grown slowly over the years, houses only several hundred yards apart might be decades older—or newer—than those on our street, and look "foreign" even to our untrained eyes.

We also came to sense that the mixture of occupations represented on a single block often contradicted the supposed makeup of residential divisions around town. On our own street, there was a doctor, banker, engineer, used car dealer, newspaper editor, sign painter, factory worker, retired jeweler, grocery store owner, deliveryman, schoolteacher, and tinsmith. This variety led to a certain democratic spirit among neighbors, including us kids, who had playmates from many backgrounds. Reinforcing this early egalitarianism was the fact that nearly every youngster went to the same public high school and that many stayed in town after graduation. It wasn't odd to see a local lawyer or businessman deep in conversation with an old classmate who now pumped gas and repaired cars at the local service station.

Thus, we rarely saw the sort of rigid social segregation that plagued many metropolitan areas, where Social Registers and exclusive clubs created something approaching an upper caste. We knew that social differences existed within and among the various neighborhoods, but we also knew that the lines were not too rigid in a town where, for the most part, easy friendship and mutual respect began in childhood and could last for a lifetime. Sadly, this general comradery did not extend to the few Black families in town who all lived in one small neighborhood just east of downtown.

Our ubiquitous front porches in the North End, and in many other parts the community, reinforced friendly feelings. Only later did we discover that our cheerful front porches were leftovers of the nineteenth-century Romantic belief that nature was a sort of friend and partner in creation. The porch was a way of pushing the house out into nature, where the whole family could enjoy the out-of-doors in domestic comfort. When we were growing up, before anyone in our part of the country really thought about the luxury of air conditioners, the shade of a wide front porch was one of the best places to cool off. We spent many summer nights there, talking to parents and catching lightning bugs, or counting the cars that drove by. Walking up and down the street, we could hear the low murmur of conversation, punctuated with bursts of laughter, as families and friends "whiled away" the warm hours before bedtime out on the porch. Our porches were a palpable contrast to a later suburban way of life, where people enter their houses through a garage and spend their free time in the backyard or on the back patio, hidden away from both neighbors and the passing traffic.

Most of our porches reached across the whole front of the house, and sometimes they bent around one side of the structure, resulting in the much-admired L-shaped porch. The porches were entirely made of wood, from the heavy round posts and encircling railings to the blue-grey floorboards and white or light-blue wooden ceilings. Reflecting our parents' devotion to these outdoor appendages were the hours they spent each summer keeping them neat and clean. They often spent a whole weekend in May washing down the porch with buckets of suds and scrub brushes. For the rest of the summer our mothers swept the porch every day or two with a good stiff broom. In fact, having a well-swept porch, in addition to a clean sidewalk, was a sign of middle-class respectability all over town. Homemakers who couldn't manage this task were thought to be lazy, inconsiderate, or both.

Connecting houses in the neighborhood as well as joining neighborhoods to one another—and nearly everyone to the downtown—was a network of sidewalks. These pedestrian pathways and the relatively short distances from one part of town to the other echoed the walking scale of our community. This arrangement was a liberating feature for older kids who could walk on their own to visit friends and relatives and take themselves to the public library or to the movies. They could also walk to school and many accompanied their families on foot to church. (The growing car culture and the appearance of suburban developments on the edges of even our town, along with the shopping centers and various drive-through facilities that catered to those on wheels, would undermine this walking scale in the years ahead and contribute to environmental pollution and eventually to climate change.)

Nearly all the houses surrounding us were made of wood, and usually painted white. Since those on our street dated from the early 1900s, most of them belonged to a transitional style. With their large rooms and high ceilings, they looked back to the spaciousness of the late Victorian dwelling, but their simple lines reflected the Colonial Revival that we later learned was emerging at the time. Some of these houses even had crude Palladian windows in the attic story as a sign of their debt to the Colonial and neoclassical past. However, such interpretations remained a mystery in childhood, since neither we or our parents knew anything about the Colonial Revival, let alone the Venetian architect, Andrea Palladio, and his great impact on Anglo-American architecture.

Shade trees—most of them maples of one variety or another—that had grown as tall as rooftops by the time we appeared on the scene, were a visual relief to our boxy white houses. These trees lined both sides of the street and created a shady, green arcade from one intersection to the next. Most of the yards were also "landscaped" to some extent, though nobody would have used that word. None of our neighbors dreamed of joining a garden club—or of hiring a landscape designer for advice on how to improve the yard. Instead, they relied on common sense, casual observation, and perhaps a few tips from a neighbor who was reputed to have a "green thumb."

In practice, this meant that we had four or five bushes in the front yard just below and along the porch. For the most part, these were badly spaced and often scraggly—especially around houses where shade trees blocked direct sunlight. In backyards, where there were not so many trees, there might be flowering shrubs, such as lilacs, forsythia, or roses. These backyard plantings had a random look that came from an inadvertent lack of planning. At the far end of our backyards there were family vegetable gardens, unambitious patches of tomatoes, green peppers, and weeds. Along many side fences, there were equally unambitious flower beds with a few bulbs and common perennials that shared space with whatever our parents picked up at the local "greenhouse"— our universal term for any sort of nursery or garden shop. Some neighbors put up board fences to separate their backyards from the alley behind, planting hollyhocks along them to hide ugly, graying boards. The hollyhocks came up in a riot of tropical colors in early summer but were beaten down by the first good thunderstorm and looked even worse in late summer as the tall stalks dried, cracked, and bent down to the ground.

Our parents and neighbors approached interior decoration in the same amateurish, nonchalant way that they tended their backyards and flowerbeds. Few coordinated furniture styles or color schemes. Instead, they decorated rooms with pieces of furniture from local stores as they could afford them. Most of the inside walls sported wallpaper, including the ceilings, while chairs and sofas (called davenports in our "neck of the woods") appeared in whatever style happened to be "in" when purchased. Often home decoration reflected popular styles at the time when its owners had married and "gone to housekeeping" (a euphemism to deemphasize the sexual side of marriage).

We noticed especially that the homes of older couples appeared hopelessly old fashioned. One of these homes belonged to a couple we knew as Mom and Pop Smith, retired owners of a jewelry store who by then were plump, white-haired, and in their eighties. In their old-fashioned parlor, we found heavy velvet curtains hanging from the double doorway that divided the "front room" from a more casual sitting room next to it. In one corner of this first room was a dark upright piano, covered on top with a fringed cloth and faded, framed photographs. In our own houses, there were upholstered chairs and sofas in a Grand Rapids version of supposed colonial styles, along with a family heirloom or two unconsciously plunked down wherever they seemed to fit. The results were far from elegant, but they were usually warm and friendly.

As much as we appreciated the comfort of the house's main rooms, two completely undecorated parts of the house could hold our interests for hours at a time, especially on rainy days. These were basements and attics. Since one corner of the basement contained the washing machine and, in another corner, Dad's workbench, the attic was more remote and less vulnerable to intrusion by adults. In the barn-like older houses of our childhoods, the attic was a large, steeply pitched, high-ceilinged space that ran the whole length and width of the house. These attics were so big that we could use them as wintertime shooting galleries for BB guns, with old, framed pictures of long departed family members offering the most tempting targets. Once we converted an attic into a movie studio where we staged and shot our own western thriller with a cheap, hand-held 8-millimeter movie camera. The best part of the set was a wild-west saloon, complete with an old mirror and used whiskey bottles filled with colored water.

The attic was also a place where we sometimes felt in touch with earlier generations of the family, since it contained old furniture and clothes, as well as dusty trunks full of diplomas, books, old letters, and postcards, and other "odds and ends." Then there might be a few items left behind by earlier owners of the house whose children, we imagined, had once played in the same attic, and had slept in our bedrooms below. We also sensed a kind of timeless quality about the attic that was unmarked by the waves of contemporary furniture which had passed through the downstairs part of the house with each owner. Up in the attic on a rainy afternoon we could feel connected in some

mysterious way to everyone who had lived in the house
before we happened on the scene.

Sometimes a dusty object in the attic evoked a
much wider world, as when we stumbled across a yellowed
and crumbling fragment of our local newspaper from
March 1938. Thinking about this date led us to imagine
what the news had conveyed of our town on that day—and
of a world that was already moving toward war.

We also felt connected through everyday neighborhood sounds. We awakened to the rhythms of chirping birds, the whir of the milk truck as it made its way slowly down the street, and to the clang of heavy glass milk bottles plunked down on the front porch. Summer afternoons came with the sounds of yelling kids, barking dogs, and car tires as they rippled down the brick streets and bounced over a manhole cover, which plunked back into place with a dull metallic thud. Just before supper we heard the high-pitched calls of moms trying to round up their broods for the evening meal, served in most families at exactly six o'clock.

The most comforting sounds came on summer or early autumn nights as we lay in bed trying to fall asleep. Crickets sang outside the window, interrupted by the muffled tones of the town clock announcing each hour. From over on the West Side, we heard the freight trains as they slid through town, blowing their mournful whistles at every crossing until the last, barely audible sounds dissolved into the heavy night air. Best of all was the sound of a father's car as he pulled into the driveway after an evening meeting with some civic group downtown. The car sat for a moment, idling on the cement as he pulled open the heavy wooden garage door. The car door slammed again, and the motor heaved in one last effort of the day as it passed into the musty interior of the garage. Then came Dad's strong and certain footsteps as he rounded the house, and if it were not too late, pausing below our open bedroom window to a say a cheery goodnight.

Other happy feelings stemmed from the neighborliness up and down the street. We knew everyone on the block. Some of the families, including our own, had lived in the neighborhood for decades. While not all the adults were close friends, they at least knew each other's names and talked along sidewalks or over backyard fences. As a result, people who moved in from other sections of town or from other towns and states could strike us almost like foreigners at first. One boy, who eventually became a good friend, arrived from Florida after having spent his earlier years in Minnesota. His father, who was a professional photographer, had supposedly pulled out a map one day, blindly jabbed his finger on the spot marking our town, and decided to move his family there. Such a slapdash method of deciding where to live strikes us as odd even now, but back then it seemed like a type of madness.

Of course, we learned about a few neighborhood feuds. One, between two women who lived across the street from each other, lasted until death. It began when a cousin of one of the women died and space was not reserved for her in the "family car," a large black Cadillac which all the funeral directors maintained for driving families from the funeral home—or church—to the cemetery. After the funeral, the two women never spoke to each other again. Both admitted to our moms that they wanted to patch things up, but each was too stubborn to make the first move—or was maybe afraid their overtures would meet with scorn.

We knew of another ongoing argument between an angry old man up the street and a neighbor woman. We never knew what it was all about, but with a kid's twisted sense of humor, we loved to see the old fellow spit a huge wad of chewing tobacco all over the woman's front porch and steps, something he seemed to do about once a month.

Another conflict, involving a young husband accused of wife beating, genuinely terrified us. The police came and converged on the dwelling, an upstairs apartment in an old house. We stood in fascinated fear as our local finest arrayed themselves behind trees and under the outside staircase while the crazed husband, brandishing a pistol, stood at the top of the steps shouting great heaving obscenities about his wife's unfaithfulness and the perfidy of women in general. Somehow, the police managed to take him without firing a shot. For several weeks afterward the neighborhood women confessed to one another that they knew the woman had been "slipping around," or as local matrons put it, "had all the morals of Liz Taylor's cat."

"But with a husband like that," they added, "It was no wonder."

It was our neighborhood women who stayed home all day, at a time when few worked outside the home, and who set the local standards of behavior. If a neighbor had the reputation as a tippler or was thought to look over-long at young girls passing by, they warned us darkly to stay away from his yard.

Cooperation in our neighborhood went beyond such negative issues. The women often looked after each other's kids, allowing a young mother to run off to the grocery store, and at times of sickness and death, they prepared a hot meal for the stricken family. When there was a death in the neighborhood, someone volunteered to go around to families up and down the street and to collect small amounts of cash for a joint flower arrangement. And seldom did our mothers hesitate—in fact thought it their duty—to correct a child who was misbehaving away from home.

The neighborhood women also kept each other company during these years after the war when the men had come back and wanted their wives out of the work force, supposedly safe and secure at home. Most of the women agreed that their proper place was at home, though their daughters would have very different ideas only a few years later. We can imagine, all over town, women visiting after "their men" had left for work and they had finished the morning chores. Often with children under foot, they played cards, canned fruits and vegetables, darned socks, and knitted sweaters, and supported each other with spirited talk. One woman on the block was famous for showing up at a neighbor's house on hot summer mornings with a small, six-and-a-half-ounce bottle of Coke and proposing to split it. Since we knew her as a delightful if sometimes-wacky neighbor, stories of her thrifty habits good-naturedly made the rounds of the neighborhood and entered family legend.

There was another woman up the street, an attractive divorcee, and the mother of a young son, who had to go off to work every day. She was a bit notorious for her habit on hot summer nights of ironing clothes in her living room wearing only a bra and panties, while leaving the front door open in hopes of catching a cool breeze. Yet the other women trusted her and could joke about how all the neighborhood men seemed to get restless on those warm nights and made excuses like having to walk the dog just so they could pass ever so slowly past her house.

Besides walking the dog, the men pitched in to help each other. They collaborated to install new TV antennas or fix a plumbing problem. When we had a big snow, they all pulled together to dig out the street. The most exciting case of this teamwork came during one famous blizzard, when Mother Nature dumped nearly three feet of snow on us and whipped it into drifts over six feet high.

We were snowed in for days. Neighbors shared food and spent much of the day sledding, walking through the narrow white canyons the men had carved out along the sidewalks, and complained cheerfully about the terrible weather. We remembered the snug friendliness of that week for years, and secretly hoped that another blizzard

might come along
and let us relive that
very special time. It
never did.

On a less
exciting level, our
neighborhood men
might run into each
other at a nearby gas
station, sometimes
just walking down
to buy a cigar or

pack of cigarettes. On weekends and during the summer
months we also walked or rode our bikes to the station to
buy a bottle of pop (soda out East) from a low, dark red
cooler filled with ice-cold water. The water was so cold that
it made our fingers numb after only a few seconds of
fishing around for a favorite drink. On the wall above the
cooler was an old radio that gave out as much static as
music or news reports, which owner Ralph Archer and the
assorted male loafers vaguely listened to, perking up their
ears whenever something caught their attention. It was
from this radio one autumn afternoon that several of us

learned about the ruthless, Soviet suppression of the Hungarian uprising. It was on a similar radio in another gas station during a Sunday afternoon in early December where one of our dads heard the grim announcement of Japan's bombing of Pearl Harbor and knew in an instant that he would soon be in the service.

Some of our other favorite gathering places were the neighborhood grocery stores. Although there were already a few supermarkets in town, many women still could not drive and frequently used these walk-in stores. One of them, owned by a Mr. Rickets (who did not appear to have a first name), was only a block away from our house. Going there from a very early age with our mothers, we couldn't remember a time when its matter-of-fact proprietor was anything but a fixture in the neighborhood. Of indeterminate age, Rickets was a slender man whose otherwise pale and plain face was marked by wire-rimmed bifocals, a deep cleft in his chin, and a cluster of small red blood vessels on the surface of each cheek. He wore a pair of dark wool pants and a well-worn cardigan sweater that was as drab as the rest of his outfit. During the war, he hid bananas behind the marble-topped, wooden counter for moms, since he worried that babies and toddlers in the neighborhood might not have enough fresh fruit to eat. When we were five or six years old, our moms sent us up to his place on our first errand into the outside world. Mr. Rickets seemed to know that we were coming (doubtless because of a hasty telephone call from home) and he went out of his way to make this first solo visit a happy experience.

Yet another of these informal gathering places was a drugstore about five blocks away, whose soda fountain was an attraction for all ages. Its specialty was a dark, syrupy, fountain Coke, served in a cone-shaped paper cup, held upright in a shiny metal holder. We were fascinated to see how the server picked up one of these cups, actually a paper liner, by slamming the metal holder upside down onto a stack of them and making use of the suction thus created to bring up the holder and just one-liner—now joined.

Bolting through the drugstore's front door, we ran over to the counter and plopped down on one of the red swivel stools. Since this was bound to aggravate the adult customers as well as to make sure we would spill our drinks all over the counter, our mothers made us sit with them near the back of the store at one of the several tables with see-through glass tops. There, an aging, and understandably irritated waitress served us. Shuffling back and forth in carpet slippers, she had bleached hair and a withered face caked with cheap, dime-store make-up. We kids were always a little scared of her (and only in retrospect can we feel sorry for the pinched life she must have lived).

These visits to the drugstore were part of our everyday lives. So were the men, women, and children in the neighborhood, which consisted of four whole generations. The oldest neighbor, born in 1860, could remember, as a five-year-old girl, the church bells ringing all over town to mark the end of the Civil War. Just a decade or so younger were Mom and Pop Smith. The Smiths had no children of their own (for reasons that they never explained) and for several generations they more or less "adopted" every kid in the neighborhood. In our parents' time, they threw watermelon parties for all the children on the block. However, they were best known for the red candy hearts they continued to turn out by the hundreds every Valentine's Day. These were hard, sugary candies, flavored with oil of cinnamon and oil of sassafras, and measured about four inches across and an inch thick. They could keep us occupied for most of a day.

We connected these older residents with our grandparents, and they sometimes played the part to kids whose own grandparents had died or lived far away. Even for adults whose mothers or fathers had died, these older neighbors sometimes filled the void. When our maternal grandmother died, our mothers looked to Mom Smith for some of the advice and emotional support their mother had given them. The fact that Mom Smith and our grandmother had been good friends and neighbors made our ongoing relationship with her all the closer.

Of course, there were folks in our end of town who didn't fit any of the familiar types. The best term for them is "characters," memorable eccentrics whose influence was tangential at best, yet whose lives and peculiar behavior revealed a rich culture of individuals who didn't dress in suits or even work with any obvious regularity. We knew one of them as "Ring Neck." He was a heavy, middle-aged man who drove a long green Studebaker. His girth was such that he had to push the front seat back as far as it would go, making his huge profile especially visible from the rear window. His most terrifying feature, and the one we liked the best, was a deep scar around his throat, the result, we believed, of a vicious knife fight years before.

We heard he had once belonged to the Mafia in Chicago and had been a good friend of Al Capone. We never wondered why he would be oiling his way around our streets after the excitement of gangland murders in the Windy City. Whoever Ring Neck really was, something that we never did discover, he was probably harmless. Our moms were not about to take any chances, though, and warned us darkly, "Just stay away from him."

Almost as interesting was a man we called "Dirty Joe," another character whose real name and origins we never knew. Old Joe lived in a shack in the county fairgrounds where he made a bare living by cleaning out horse stalls. Our parents were mildly worried that he might be dangerous, but "only the police know for sure," they said. Such veiled warnings about Joe only urged us on to acts of bravery like riding our bikes past his shack after dark. We heard stories of how curses, flying bottles, and strange footsteps had greeted other intruders, but we never encountered anything more than an eerie silence during these nocturnal visits. (As we look back, he was another fellow resident who deserved understanding instead of mockery.)

Then there was Mrs. Brumbaugh, one of our babysitters. She was a thin, bony woman who always brought a harmonica to entertain us. Her other famous characteristic was a set of loose false teeth which she also exploited for their entertainment value: she would open her mouth wide, unleash an inhuman wail, and let her upper teeth drop off the gums as we stared in awe.

Other characters in our wider neighborhood included a former drum player who liked to walk the streets pretending that he was a railroad engine, making chugging noises with his mouth and moving his arms back and forth to imitate the action of pistons and flywheels. Sometimes he put the make-believe choo-choo into reverse and chugged backwards down the pavement, puffing and flailing as he moved along, and ignoring the curious stares.

Then there was a bus driver who suffered, we surmised many years later, from some sort of lung problem. As we rode along in the bus, we thought his long deep coughs harmonized perfectly with the bus's wheezing old engine and grinding gears, sounds punctuated by the driver's sudden spitting out the window. Unwary riders might be showered through the open back windows when the driver let go a glob of shiny mucous. Although the poor man suffered miserably, he became an object of high imitation to us kids who loved to play bus diver at home, complete with imaginary coughing, shifting of gears, and "hocking" out the window, yet another act of childish insensitivity.

Our most vivid memories are of Henry Weaver Davidson, a man of indeterminate age and great size, with a splendid beard at a time when facial hair of any kind was considered eccentric. We invariably saw him pushing a homemade cart around the streets, which he used to pick up bottles and scrap, an activity that was supposed to have made him a millionaire. We also heard that he was a poet and inventor of great fame who chose to walk around the streets collecting trash as a way of thumbing his nose at wealth and the social position that went with it. His greatest invention, we heard, was a tube running from the seat of a car or truck down through the floorboards. The tube let drivers "pee" as they sped along, saving them the time and inconvenience of having to stop to relieve themselves. As with most of the other characters, we never did discover the truth about Henry's strange life, and probably would have been disappointed if we knew the details. In his case, the fact that we could pass along such admiring information about this strange duck showed a healthy respect for him, as well as for some of the other eccentrics. (In truth, we later learned that Henry had inherited a comfortable sum of money from his successful lawyer father and just seemed to enjoy the role of an eccentric.)

Besides these characters, there were several men and women, all of them associated with the healing professions, who stand out in our memories. One of them, a "Dr. Hodge," who was a neighborhood

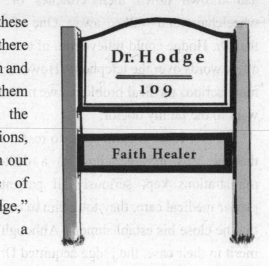

faith healer who had never spent a day of his life in medical school, but whose renown spread over several counties. Every day his waiting room, and frequently during the summer months, his front porch and sidewalk, overflowed with afflicted men and women. We saw them waiting, often with gnarled faces and twisted limbs, hoping against hope for a miracle cure in the hands of Dr. Hodge. We felt sorry for them but often avoided passing the place, repelled by such monstrous suffering, and feeling that Hodge's house was more than a little spooky. Still, we were attracted to the place because of stories about patients who had thrown down their crutches or jumped out of wheelchairs and walked away. One of our uncles swore that Dr. Hodge could relieve him of a sore throat with just a few words over the telephone. However, when it came to more serious medical problems, we noticed that he always went to the family doctor.

Our local doctors came to resent Hodge. Charging that he was masquerading as a doctor and that his ministrations kept seriously ill patients from seeking proper medical care, they took him to court and demanded that he close his establishment. Although there was much merit to their case, the judge acquitted Dr. Hodge because it was his patients, and not he who called himself a doctor. Nor did he charge professional fees, relying instead on whatever donations his visitors left in a basket on the hall table. Some of our neighbors, who were tired of the pretensions of local doctors, applauded the decision and congratulated Hodge on his victory.

Our own family practitioner was a man in late middle age who lived several doors down the street and was at our beck and call. We could walk down to his house when we saw his car was out front; or if we really felt rotten, he would slip over to see us. In the case of a childhood illness that lasted several days, he stopped by our house on his way home from the office to dinner. He never seemed to be in a hurry and took his time examining us, talking absentmindedly as he unpacked his black bag and went through his routine. Most interesting were the little bottles of different colored pills that lined the sides of his bag. If indicated, he poured a handful of tablets into a small white envelope and slowly wrote on the front in his indecipherable script how many we were supposed to take each day. Then he licked the flap and pasted shut the little packet of pills. Of course, we were always on the lookout for him to pull a hypodermic needle from the bag to give us a dreaded shot.

The suspense over whether we would get a shot could last for a half hour or more, as the doctor watched TV with us and was never in a hurry to get home, at least until his wife called and ordered him home. Our parents told us later that the doctor and his wife had a stormy marriage and that he stalled as long for as he could before leaving to "face the music."

Our parents also knew that this neighbor/doctor was an excellent diagnostician who, with his experienced eyes, ears, and hands, made an on-the-spot diagnosis that was usually confirmed, if necessary, in the hospital or at the laboratory. He also brought many of us into the world and watched us grow up in the neighborhood. He knew each household well, including the emotional strains that were as important to good health as a strong constitution and a healthy diet. Bedside manners came naturally to this man whom we liked as a friend and neighbor as well as our doctor.

Rounding out our neighborhood medical establishment were the Howe sisters, two public health nurses who lived together as "maiden ladies" in a small cottage in the woods at the foot of the Fresh Air Camps. They had come to town from Boston, Massachusetts, a generation before and looked after the poorer inhabitants of the community, in addition to supervising the summer youth camp up the hill from the back of their house. Unable to drive a car, or probably to afford one, they took the bus or walked to see widely scattered people in need. Wherever they went, we saw them in their stiffly starched blue uniforms and caps. This garb and their serious faces made them look like severe New England schoolteachers, but we knew these stern looks masked kind hearts that went out to less fortunate folks. We were surprised after their deaths to learn that they had been taken back to Boston for burial in the fashionable Mount Auburn Cemetery, causing us to think they might have belonged to that city's famous Howe family.

Through our neighborhood—with its familiar sights and sounds and with its many characters—we gained a sense of security and place. Nevertheless, for the most fortunate of us, our families gave us the strongest sense of who we were while growing up.

3. The Family Web

Spouses have spent years trying to figure out the family network. We've tried explaining family trees, and even pulled out old photo albums, identifying all the main characters and how they're connected. However, we gave up hope long ago that they'd ever fit all the pieces together. So, we'll start by saying that our family included more than a dozen cousins—plus aunts, uncles, grandparents, great-grandparents, and in-laws on all sides. We spent holidays together, handed down tribal memories, and despite some failings, shared a genuine emotional cement.

Although both sides of our family were important, our mothers' kin made the greatest impact. There were seven of them growing up together, six girls, including our mothers, and one boy. The brother married a girl from a nearby village, while four of the sisters, our two mothers (and two aunts), married local guys. Two other sisters married men from other parts of the state. Most important for us were the five siblings who stayed in or around town to raise their families; and because they lived nearby, we all felt very close.

The early deaths of our maternal grandparents led our mothers, aunts, and one uncle, to lean on one another, to varying degrees, for emotional support. The fact that six of them were girls only added to a close-knit family since women made most of the social arrangements. If the mixture of boys and girls had been the other way around, we doubt that their "in-law" wives would have tried so hard to keep in touch.

In addition to our extended family's being a thriving internal success, our fathers and uncles (by blood and by marriage) were fortunate enough to hold down middle-class jobs. Our grandfather had owned a furniture store on the West Side of town, where he catered to the tastes of local, blue-collar families. Our mothers' only brother inherited the furniture business. The sisters' husbands eventually found jobs as a bank president, newspaper editor, druggist, car dealer, metallurgist, and trucking company executive. None of them would qualify as wealthy, but they managed to support their families in modest comfort as the only breadwinner.

These aunts, uncles, and parents belonged to the third and we to the fourth generation of living family members. Our great-grandparents came into the world during the 1860s and lived through the Civil War or its immediate aftermath as small children, while our grandparents were born during the late 1800s. Our grandparents, as youngsters, had grown up in the pre-automobile age—in fact, "pre-everything" we thought, from inside toilets, electric lights, and telephones to airplanes flying overhead.

In some ways, we suspected that these older relatives suffered from a life-long culture shock. They often associated the many new marvels with dramatic personal events, such as their first ride in a car or maiden conversation over the telephone. One of our grandmothers, who grew up in the country, took her first car ride after a long day at the county fair. She and her parents missed the last train home and had to "hire a machine" to drive them the seven or eight miles back to the farm. Grandma was so excited that she couldn't get to sleep for hours that night, and every time she told the story, it seemed as full of childhood awe as when it had happened.

Grandma's first experience with the telephone was about 1914, and they had to share a party line with eight other families. The instrument was one of those large, wooden boxes that hung on the wall and had a crank on one side they had to turn several times to get the operator. The party line allowed them to listen secretly to all their neighbor's conversations and that way take in the gossip for miles around. She or her sister would stand for hours in front of the box with one hand over the mouthpiece so that no one could tell she was eavesdropping. When she couldn't stand for another second, she carefully hung up the receiver, sat down at the kitchen table with a sigh, and spent another hour or two relaying all the juicy tidbits to the rest of the family.

We are sometimes amazed to realize that we once knew men and women who would now be over 150 years old. Perhaps we are the last generation to have "touched" those men and women who lived through that great transition from an older world of horses and only face-to-face or written communication to a world of automobiles, airplanes, telephones, TV—and, more ominously, to the possible annihilation of all humanity through nuclear war. Through their stories, we gained an "extended memory" that went well before our entrances into the world.

One modernism our elders did not "cotton to," or even try to understand, was Freudian psychology—or any other version of mental analysis. To them, "ego" meant arrogance, while the "unconscious" was what happened when someone fell and banged her head and blacked out. Thus, when we later tried to discuss our own personality quirks, they often responded defensively and testily, "Your grandfather was exactly the same way." Chances are that Grandpa was not "exactly the same way" but bringing up a relative's name and alleged personality served as a familiar incantation they hoped would exorcize the problem by making it seem normal, at least for the time being. They also pointed to the hardships of farm life or the Great Depression as examples of how we, too, could overcome adversity by sheer grit and family example, rather than through what they liked to call the "mumbo-jumbo" of psychotherapy.

They also trotted out examples from family members who had passed into the great beyond, sometimes in answer to a personal problem, and sometimes as a reaffirmation of who we were. In case we forgot, visits with parents to the local cemetery helped to joggle the mind. These treks to the "marble orchard" were far from morbid affairs and more like family outings. We walked the few blocks to the cemetery, located on a steep hill at the edge of town. As we moved from grave to grave, pulling up weeds or arranging flowers, we heard little stories about grandparents, great-grandparents,  or even a neighbor who had died. It was during these curiously sweet moments that we learned of our maternal grandfather's hot temper and how he had supposedly knocked a dentist down his office stairs for pulling the wrong tooth, a dubious story much embellished over the years. We also heard how, in his loneliness after our grandmother died, he went out into the back yard and talked to the chickens (which caused his grandchildren, us cousins, to call him "Chee Chee" in imitation of how we thought the chickens sounded). In this way, the cemetery became an almost cheerful extension of the family, a place where we also played or hiked on our own, feeling that we were among kindly souls.

However, such stories were not reserved for the cemetery. Over and over, references to an ancestor subtly reinforced our sense of place and of belonging. One of these was about a grandfather who came to the United States from Italy when he was only18 to escape the limited opportunities of a beautiful but poor hill town in Calabria. He went on to become the supervisor, or "padrone," of a gang of men who laid gas pipes across the countryside, camping at the worksite during the summers. During one of these encampments, he met a farm girl whose ancestors were Pennsylvania Dutch farmers who had migrated west three generations before. They were married a year later.

One of our grandmothers arrived in town from Indiana as a gospel singer and made her move on a young bachelor doctor, whom she married and "rode herd on" for the rest of his life. We heard these courtship tales more times than we can remember, and figured, without really being told, that out of these ancient passions had come our own flesh and blood. Each of these stories added yet another chapter to our inner library of self-identity.

Of course, it was the generation just above us, consisting of parents, uncles, and aunts, who made the greatest impression. They had been born in the teens and twenties of the last century and were young survivors of the Great Depression and World War II. Although born a quarter century or so before us, their childhood experiences became woven into our own.

Our uncles were the first adult men we knew besides our own fathers. Uncle Walter was the most laid-back man we ever encountered. A local car dealer, he was familiar with every mechanic and car salesman in the county; and on family drives, or even on the way to family gatherings, he stopped at gas stations to spend a few minutes with other men who loved and knew cars. Uncle Perrin was a reporter and later the editor of our local newspaper. We remember him as an enthusiastic discusser of history and current events, and as the owner of the largest private library in the family. As the father of three sons, he looked forward to family gatherings where he could kid his young nieces. His one aberration was a fanatical devotion to the state university's football team. A loyal alumnus, he spent Saturday mornings before the game blasting the university fight song from a record player and running around the house in his old raccoon coat, singing along with the music and waving pennants. He was inconsolable when the team lost, and we all avoided saying anything to him for several hours—or even several days— after such a tragedy.

Uncle Miles was a genuine war hero and had the medals to prove it, including the Distinguished Flying Cross, but we only saw them when his wife, Aunt Betty, took them out. In the dark recesses of his bedroom closet, we could find everything from leather flying jackets, regimental patches, and a .45 caliber pistol to a dusty dress uniform covered with battle ribbons and dog-eared snapshots of Army Air Corps buddies clowning around in front of tents in New Guinea, the Philippines, or Okinawa. Sometimes we noticed Uncle Miles standing on the front porch at family events with the other men, his hands rising, falling, and arching through the air as he recalled a close scrape with a Japanese pilot, or how his plane had been riddled with flack, and how he dive-bombed enemy shipping in the South China Sea. Although it was not his intention, these stories made us feel that World War II was an exciting and even romantic adventure—a puzzling contradiction to the picture of a grim contest painted by cold warriors in the 1950s.

Our Uncle Dave thrilled us with windy trips in the back of his pickup truck—or with speedboat rides from his cottage at the lake. He was also the uncle who passed out nickels and dimes, and who excited our sense of wickedness by telling dirty jokes with us in the room.

Uncle Jim and Uncle Harold had the best dry wits, talents we appreciated only later. Uncle Harold, who was the oldest of the uncles by marriage, liked to tell stories of how he and three friends had put together a poor excuse for a jazz band in the 1920s but managed anyway to land a gig one summer in a French resort town. To their French audiences, all agog over this new American sound, any band from the States sounded terrific. And there was Uncle Tom who treated us to big-league baseball games. We also marveled at his ability to eat barely cooked steaks and then wash them down with several packets of antacid tablets.

Even our great uncles and their families could be instructive. Through Uncle Arthur, our maternal grandfather's older brother, we experienced a real connection with farm life. His family were a gentle, churchgoing, hardworking lot, who kidded us about our city-slicker ways. This was a laugh since our town was as much like a real city as a shaft of wheat is like a tree.

Uncle Arthur's children were about the same age as our parents, and we were about the same age as his grandchildren, our second cousins. The boys impressed us with their *can-do* ways, so typical of farmers' sons. With just string, bailing wire, or whatever they found around the place, they could fix most anything—or hot-wire a car or truck. Because they learned to work tractors as kids, driving was nothing for them, while we town boys had to wait until 16 to sit behind a wheel.

We usually saw our second cousins once a year, when we had a huge family reunion at Uncle Arthur's farm, which was an annual coming together of the town and country sides of our mothers' family. The farm men were sunburned and ropey, our fathers pale and out of shape. Their women were bigger and less fashionable than our mothers were, with rough square hands and no-nonsense clothing. But we didn't let any of this get in the way of a good time. After a few awkward minutes, the women started trading recipes or knitting patterns, while the men talked about the latest farm subsidies or labor disputes in town. We chased each other through the big, two-story bank barn, examined cow's teats, and argued about baseball statistics.

We all looked forward to the huge farm dinner at noon, eaten under the trees on long tables that were made of heavy wooden planks placed between sawhorses. For dessert, there was sweet, rich ice cream that began with Uncle Arthur's cows and was finished off in old-fashioned wooden freezers filled with chipped ice that we churned with a crank. At first, it was easy to turn the paddles through the runny mixture, but as it began to harden, our arms gave out and we had to turn the job over to our country cousins who jibed at our weak "city" arms.

These visits to the farm left some of us dazzled by all the living creatures and complex implements we had only known from picture books or had seen as we whizzed down country roads in the family car. The trip home was full of talk about cows, hogs, chickens, ducks, tractors, plows, combines, and other assorted objects of awe. Even as winter began, we had not forgotten the farm, and begged Santa, and then our parents, for a new "farm set" on Christmas.

Another great uncle—also our maternal grandfather's brother—was Uncle Eli. He was an ordained Presbyterian minister who in 1910 had gone straight from seminary to Korea where he was a missionary for 30 years until the U.S. State Department warned him to leave because of deteriorating relations with Japan, which had made Korea into a Japanese colony. While there, he became president of Soongsil College (now University). In 1919, he supported the students in their "March First" uprising against Japanese colonialism and was jailed by the Japanese authorities until the U.S. State Department secured his release. Our family gatherings must have seemed like a tame affair to him after such a full life. To us he was a remote, elderly gentleman, who sat by the fireplace quietly enjoying the noisy antics of his dead brother's grandchildren. Still, he was a kind of saintly hero to us, someone to be proud of, even if we couldn't hope to imitate him in everyday life.

However interesting the uncles— "great" or otherwise—it was the maternal aunts, who were at the center of our extended family life. Born between 1911 and 1923, with a stillborn child in between, their mother had been pregnant eight times in just eleven years—becoming something of a rarity even in those days and phenomenal in our own. Although this was a hardship to their mother, the children being so near in age had made for close ties among them. We can picture nights back in the 1920s and 1930s, with six girls romping in an upstairs bedroom, giggling about boys, hatching pranks to play on their temperamental father, and later supporting each other through breakups with boyfriends or "fallings out" with schoolmates.

It's no wonder that these aunts were like second mothers to us. The younger ones, and especially before they got married, were our favorite babysitters. If one of us got sick, our mothers consulted each other about possible diagnoses and remedies. And none of them held back from scolding us if we misbehaved when our parents weren't around—or even when they were around.

Important influences, too, were the nearly dozen-and-a-half first cousins on the maternal side. We cousins were born over a sixteen-year span, the oldest in 1936 and the youngest in 1952. Three were born before the American entry into World War II and four during the war. The other eight came during the early postwar years and were our tribe's contribution to the nation-wide baby boom.

Ten of the cousins grew up in the old hometown and were a lot like brothers and sisters. The fact that some cousins might be closer in age than a brother or sister meant they could make better playmates than the real thing. Yet there could be a degree of competition between cousins. Parents couldn't help comparing us as we grew up, though they were careful not to overdo it. In addition, we went on to measure ourselves against each other in athletic prowess and board games, and later in academic and vocational accomplishments. We might be proud of what our cousins accomplished but felt compelled to try to keep up with them, although in different ways. Mostly, none of us wanted to disappoint other family members—whether they were cousins, parents, aunts, or uncles.

It was also within this family web that we cousins tested our maturity—and our elders' patience. Some of us faced up to this moment of truth in the 1960s when we joined many other young people in bombarding our relatives with liberal, anti-war, anti-government, and anti-establishment criticism. We discovered that the only joy which could surpass that of angering aunts, uncles, and parents was the surprising discovery that they still loved us anyway. Of course, some of the cousins were too dutiful to risk such confrontations and backed away from this exhilarating experience. In this way, we were no different from many other families at the time.

About a third of our cousins were female, and there were times when cousins of the opposite sex could provide each other with an innocent introduction to romance. Some of us developed strong crushes on our out-of-town cousins whose attraction had not been spoiled by too much everyday contact. By our time, marrying a first cousin was against the law, but first cousin marriages had once been commonplace among plantation families in the South and among the upper classes in England, in both cases as a way of keeping money and property in the family. Since none of us came from great wealth, this could not have been a good excuse, even if the law still allowed first cousin marriages.

Holidays gave the extended family an excuse to get together—if we really needed an excuse. On the Fourth of July, we assembled on an aunt's large front porch to watch the parade pass by. However, Labor Day, the last of the summer holidays, failed to rally the family. Maybe we were worn-out by summer's end, or maybe the inevitability of school's opening the next morning (at a time when schools never opened before Labor Day) put a pall over the day for us kids. We were also not a "labor family," and thus the true significance of the occasion was largely lost on us.

Summers included holidays of our own making. These often took place at "the lake," a modest body of water about 15 miles north of town where our Uncle Dave maintained a cottage that had once belonged to our grandparents. There we fished off the bank or took the rowboat out to explore a nearby island. On especially warm evenings, Uncle Dave took the bigger kids in his motorboat to a sandbar where we swam under the moonlight.

Even better was a trip to the amusement park on the other side of the lake. Built in the early 1900s at the end of an interurban rail line as a tourist attraction, the park was beginning a slow decline in the postwar years, and finally died in the 1960s as prosperity and a flood of new cars took families far from home in search of summer entertainment. Yet the park was still a little exotic. A ballroom overlooking the lake had once attracted big bands like Tommy and Jimmy Dorsey and Glenn Miller, and continued to feature some lesser known, and by then, dying big bands.

At night the park, with all the lights, gaudy colors, and carnival music, could still be a place of enchantment. Hideous looking fortunetellers with sad faces frightened and thrilled us. Tough, leathery-skinned women with two-pack-a-day voices barked from their game booths. They gave out cheap plaster-of-Paris statues for the lucky ones and persuasive come-ons for kids who barely missed a prize that they desperately wanted to prove their manhood or impress a girlfriend. We often saw some young sucker blow his whole night's allowance in one of these ball-throwing bins.

In one section of the park, there were amusement rides, including a rickety, wooden roller coaster. Running it were tattooed men wearing greasy green T-shirts, with cigarettes dangling from one corner of their mouths. Already a little scared about the ride, the looks of our surly hosts did nothing to inspire confidence. Of course, it never dawned on us that the men and women working at the park, who could seem so frightening or so exotic, might have lived difficult lives of material deprivation.

Still, the lake was a magical place for us, as it had been for our moms and their sisters who had spent summers growing up there. They had learned to swim in front of the family cottage, danced with boyfriends in the lake-front ballrooms, lazed about on hot afternoons reading novels and short stories from magazines, and kissed boys on the bridge behind the cottage. Their memories blended with our own happy times at the lake and created another bond across the generations.

Without question, the most important family event was Thanksgiving. Beginning in the early 1950s, the annual Thanksgiving dinner was at one of our aunt's homes and continued to take place there for the next 50 years. The large brick house, three blocks north of downtown, contained five big bedrooms upstairs and as many spacious rooms downstairs. On Thanksgiving Day, the individual families began to show up around 11:00 in the morning. As the women gathered in the kitchen, and the men talked in the living room, we cousins went across the street to a vacant lot for an annual football game that we pompously named the Turkey Bowl. The game was just for fun, but every year there were bruised egos and brother-on-brother confrontations to the delight of cousins not embroiled in them.

The dinner itself—like all holiday and Sunday dinners in our family back then—was at 1:00 in the afternoon. The kitchen overflowed with the women putting final touches on the meal, while Uncle Walter always carved the turkey and whining children clung to mothers'

skirts. Somehow, they managed to mash the potatoes and fill serving dishes with gravy, dressing, cranberry sauce, sweet potatoes, and succotash. By then another batch of restless kids had wandered into the kitchen and had to be shooed away so the work could go on. At that point, there was some muttering among the women over why the dads were incapable, even for a few minutes, of controlling the kids while they got the dinner ready.

Between 40 and 50 adults and children sat down for the Thanksgiving feast. The kids went through the serving line first and plopped down at one of two places away from the dining room where the adults sat. The youngest cousins claimed an old wooden table in the utility room, so called because it housed the washing machine. The older cousins, meaning the teenagers, occupied the modern, Formica-topped table in one corner of the kitchen. Only then did the moms and dads and uncles and aunts (who were really one in the same, depending on which cousins described the event) finally sat down at the dining room table, which had been elongated to its greatest length possible with boards inserted in the middle. Uncle Eli, our missionary great uncle, then said grace. After his death, Uncle Perrin inherited this honor. His prayers were always sincere and carefully worded, but they were much longer than any of us in the younger generation had the patience to endure.

After dessert, the uncles lumbered off to the TV room where they settled into a long afternoon of watching football. This was the traditional Thanksgiving game at Detroit, featuring the Lions and the Green Bay Packers. It was of no great interest in our part of the country, but it was better than watching soap operas and certainly better than washing dishes. Few of the men lasted for the entire game anyway, as the heavy meal and the warm room soon put most of them to sleep. Within half an hour, we saw the heads begin to bob, only to jerk back to attention when the announcer's voice rose over an exciting play.

In retrospect, we have sometimes thought that watching the tube and then falling asleep was an acceptable way of avoiding too much familiarity among these men who had all married into the family and, in some ways, remained partial strangers to each other. Yet even among married couples, TV could be an escape from conversation and intimacy, one of the unintended negative consequences of this new visual medium. (A half century later it was smart phones that might limit real personal contact between two people sitting across from each other in a restaurant booth, who were more intent on surfing the internet or reading and writing electronic messages than talking to each other.)

There was always a chance our moms would ask the men to help with the cleanup back in the kitchen, but not a good one, since they all agreed that the kitchen was a female preserve. In the family economy of those days, both sexes believed that food, dishes, and clearing up belonged on the female side of the ledger. Because most middle-class women did not work outside the home then, they may have preferred it that way. For, if nothing else, the division of labor underlined their very real contribution to family welfare. This was certainly true of the women in our family, who thought it their duty and sacred obligation to take good care of their husbands and children. All six of the sisters inherited this idea from their mother and tried to pass it along to their own children. What they could not know is that this limited outlook would soon run into the women's movement of the 1960s, a phenomenon they neither welcomed nor understood.

Accordingly, the women went about their Thanksgiving chores with only an occasional thought that their husbands were loafing in the TV room. By midafternoon, they were ready to move into the living room to rest, or so they hoped. They set up card tables near the fireplace where they attempted to play bridge or knit—or simply relax and talk. Their peace and quiet never lasted long, as younger children interrupted, often sent by their dozing dads, whose favorite phrase in those days was, "Go ask your mother." The women generally responded to this pestering dutifully and uncomplainingly.

When we were not badgering our moms, Thanksgiving afternoon was a time for high adventure in that big house. We raced each other down the long upstairs hallway, with frequent detours into one of the rooms to crawl under or jump up and down on the beds. Or we climbed into the dusty, stand-up attic to explore early twentieth-century ball gowns and medical books that had belonged to our uncle's doctor father. The best thing about these books was that they contained some clinical drawings of male and female genitalia that, in fact, did little or nothing to enlighten us about the mysteries of love and sex.

When our wild charges through the upstairs threatened to bring the plaster down, our mothers dragooned a couple of the sleepy men into showing home movies on a bed sheet pinned to the living room curtains.

While we elbowed and kicked each other on the floor, scenes from previous family gatherings flickered onto the wavy screen. As important as the entertainment was the reinforcement of belonging to a family network that was both deep and wide. The stacks of old photo albums in the house performed a similar function.

The movies over, tension began to build again as the afternoon came to an end and we knew it was time to draw names for Christmas gifts. One of the aunts wrote the names of each cousin on slips of paper, put them into an old hat, and, with the hat held just above eye level, invited each cousin to select a name. The adults, listed on the slips as couples, repeated the process. We then had to buy a Christmas gift for whoever's name we drew. This "Pollyanna," as some families called it, was a practical response to the prospect of buying a gift for everyone in our large family. Sometimes the results were amended, as moms agreed that it would be better for cousins of a similar age and sex to exchange gifts and agreed to swap the paper name slips. We often wished this "lottery" could be rigged in other ways, since everyone knew that some cousins (really their mothers) gave better (read more expensive) presents.

About 5:30, as the November sun began to fade, the women went back to the kitchen to put out leftovers from the monstrous meal we had eaten only a few hours before. Most of us had made ourselves half-sick from the earlier gorging, but we still lined up for more, especially the desserts. This second round of feasting led to another pile of dishes for the women to wash (at a time when almost no one we knew had automatic dish washers). Of course, paper plates would have made this much easier, but our moms and aunts were against them on general principles. For them, paper plates represented a deplorable decline in domestic standards. They might be ok for a picnic, but to use then at home would make life too easy. If such shortcuts crept into daily life, they might even erode the family work ethic, threaten personal character, and be a poor example to their daughters.

Surprisingly, Christmas did not bring another daylong family feast. On Christmas, the nuclear family asserted itself, as each of our smaller families celebrated the better part of the day at home with our own individual traditions. It was also a time for the "in-law" side of the families, who usually received short shrift on the other holidays. We cousins did manage to get together on

Christmas night for a couple of hours, with the site revolving each year among the houses of aunts and uncles. It was then that the gift exchange, initiated at Thanksgiving, took place. We ran through another house; and the evening ended with a light supper featuring sloppy Joes. These were sandwiches made of ground beef, tomato sauce, and some mild seasoning, also known in our part of the country as "Spanish Hamburgers."

By eight o'clock, the party was over, and we all left for home. We knew then the finality of another Christmas and could not help feeling a little sad as we rode along in the back seat of the car. The streets were still brightly lit, the tree was still glistening in the living room, and presents were scattered all over the house, but the month-long build-up to Christmas now ended with a gaseous wheeze. Tomorrow would be another holiday from school, but it would still be just another day.

At the time, we took these family rituals for granted, and even grumbled about having to attend them as we grew older, supposing that they would go on forever.

4. Moms and Dads

The roles of our mothers and aunts were defined in many ways by their dates of birth. Coming into the world during the early decades of  the twentieth century, they belonged to a generation when very few women in our part of the country went on to any kind of higher education. Thus, the division of labor was clear: husbands were the family breadwinners and wives were the caretakers of children and home. In that sense, we grew up in a very real matriarchy. None of the women questioned this arrangement, at least openly. None of them would have thought it possible to have both a family and a professional career, as many of their daughters and still more of their granddaughters would insist on having.

Though our mothers and aunts ruled the domestic scene, each had a distinct personality. Aunt Beth was the quiet one, who managed to get her own way through a unique brand of silent stubbornness. Determined to resist concession stand robbery at the movies, she took her kids to the picture palace at the last minute, armed with a secret stash of hot dogs, pop, and potato chips. Aunt Ginny, although younger than Aunt Beth, became something of a substitute mother to her brother and five sisters after their parents died relatively young, and to us cousins she sometimes seemed more like a young grandmother than aunt. With a combination of compassion, good humor, common sense—and often a strong dash of no nonsense— she faced the worst crises with a reassuring calmness. The other sisters turned to her for advice on childrearing, or on how to deal with a difficult neighbor. If we were sick, she was the one we most wanted to see.

In contrast, our Aunt Margaret, who lived in a big city suburb in the northern part of the state, was seldom around, but we remember her constant chain smoking and jolly ways and looked forward to her semi-annual visits. Aunt Mary Ellen, on the other hand, struck as too severe and opinionated, though we later learned that these traits were defenses to protect a kind and generous soul. Aunts Betty and Patty were the beauty queen aunts, who both married fliers during the war after they had staved off scores of other suitors, one of whom had gone so far as to "buzz" the family home in his private airplane. Another Aunt Betty, the wife of our moms' only brother is well-remembered for her good business sense and such delights as potato salad, chocolate cake, and heavily sprinkled sugar toast.

At home, each of these women structured her family's lives in various ways. Some were quick to spank, at a time when spanking was more common than later, while others were horrified at the thought. There were those who took extreme care with their children's diets or followed Dr. Spock to the letter. Others took the more casual attitude of their own mother (our grandmother). One aunt banned all candy and soft drinks at the same time a sister overwhelmed her boys with hamburgers, hot dogs, and sugary soft drinks.

Still, disagreements between sisters over how to raise their children could seem sharp. Although they generally kept these opinions to themselves, unless specifically asked, there were several times when irritation over an obnoxious child prompted one of the sisters to give unwanted advice. The typical response was, "I'll raise my kids and you raise yours." To everyone's relief that was the end of it.

One issue that brought a mild division within parental ranks was television. Our parents, of course, had grown up with radio. Even the older cousins listened to such radio programs as "Superman," "Henry Aldrich," or "Bobby Benson and the B-Bar-B Ranch," and can remember how mothers tuned into afternoon soap operas like "The Romance of Helen Trent," with its unlikely plots and quavering organ music. When television came on the scene, some of our parents didn't know how to deal with it and worried about a possible hypnotic effect of the new medium, a foreshadowing of later debates over other forms of electronic media.

Aunt Beth and Uncle Walter had no such fears. They were the first in our wider family to own a TV, and, in fact, they were among the first households in town to buy a set. The screen was round and only six inches across, though they could improve it with a piece of plastic which, when draped across the screen, magnified the picture a little. The reception was poor and the programming infrequent, with hours during the day when only a test pattern appeared. At first, we watched television with them as at the movies, with the lights turned off and plenty of popcorn to munch on.

The gatherings to watch television at Aunt Beth and Uncle Walter's house were like party nights. They worked out every detail in advance, with our individual families invited at specific times and seating arrangements pre-established. The programs we watched originated in nearby cities, such as a square dance show featuring a barn decor and country music. A popular program with some of our moms was styled as an on-air "Club," hosted by a female radio, and then, television celebrity. She talked with guests, mixing it up with song and dance routines by local talent. Often, she talked intimately about herself, her only daughter, and her husband Herman, a university professor whom she portrayed as a lovable "egghead." Sometimes she took to the organ and sang a sentimental tune, which often moved both her and the audience to tears. We kids thought that the show was both "corny" and embarrassing, but her viewers were devoted, and they bought any product she recommended on air, with the result that sponsors competed hard and paid high fees for just a few seconds on the program.

The network shows came a little later, after there were means to relay signals from station to station across the country. Our parents laughed at Milton Berle, while we enjoyed *Howdy Doody*, *Roy Rogers*, and *Lassie*. News programs featured a grim reader sitting at a desk (always a man with a deep voice), with a large map behind him, in what was supposed to look like a father's den. Absent were the discussion formats that would typify news programs several decades later. And in this age before cable TV, there were only three networks, meaning that the reporters took a moderate or middling approach to conveying the news to avoid alienating both audiences and commercial sponsors. Unimagined at the time was social media as a platform for disseminating news—or for creating one's own version of the news. In many ways, the three network news programs did a better job at unbiased reporting than the plethora of voices half a century later.

In any case, within a few years, everybody in our family had bought a television, but not without worry. Every few months, usually after reading an article on the subject in *Reader's Digest* or *The Saturday Evening Post*, parents, but especially mothers, brought up the dangers of excessive viewing. In addition to the now familiar charge that television turned kids into slack-jawed babblers with no more creativity than a floor lamp, they worried about danger to our eyes and even the possibility of getting cancer from cathode rays. Still, our parents bought TVs. In addition to enjoying television themselves, they didn't want to reject the latest technology or to subject us to ridicule from other kids whose parents already had acquired televisions. In fact, they agreed with us in feeling sorry for children whose moms and dads refused to buy a TV or could not afford one. Those who lacked the money faced many other problems, but parents who refused to have a television in their home on intellectual grounds we thought were very peculiar. Perhaps, we imagined, they had gone to some Ivy League school and had moved into town from the East. In the last analysis, our moms and dads shared the prevailing postwar view that the latest technology meant progress and that progress was good for everyone.

Contrary to parental fears, television did not consume all our energies, give us cancer, or ruin our eyesight. Fortunately, our parents read to us when we were little, and later took us to the library to borrow books. Much later, we later realized that other youngsters in town were not so fortunate, deprived of ever seeing books around the house.

We were also crazy about comic books, with "Superman" and "Batman" leading the list. Classic comic books, cartoon versions of serious literature, were never very popular but came in handy when we had to write book reports in school. Later, some of us became fans of adventure books featuring Chip Hilton or the Hardy Boys, hardcover copies of which sold for around a dollar. The earlier volumes in these series dated from our dads' childhoods, something that we noticed from the pen and ink drawings, which showed Frank and Joe Hardy tearing around Bayport in cars from the 1920s. These books have been in print for nearly a century (now revised and updated) and became a link among the generations. They will never rank as great literature, but they allowed us, and millions of other boys, to identify with the imaginative and self-reliant ways of these two teenage detectives.

We also played card games like Authors or Old Maid and spent many rainy afternoons around a Monopoly board. Another pastime was trading baseball cards, a hobby later invaded by serious collectors. For us, the thin slab of pink bubble gum that came with the cards was almost as important as the pictures themselves. The cards also gave us practice in memorization during the summer months, as we tried to impress our friends by reciting batting averages and other statistics from the backs of the cards, an almost unconscious feat that would have impressed our teachers who had a lot harder time getting us to remember spelling words or history dates. We would be rich if we could sell all those penny cards today. Maddeningly, they all disappeared in a long-ago spring housecleaning.

The family drive was yet another diversion, typically on a Sunday afternoon or on summer evenings. Ours were usually unplanned outings, suggested when we got "squirrelly" and one of our parents said, "Let's take a ride." We often asked a grandparent, great aunt, or elderly neighbor to go along, the presumption being that they did not "get out very often." We took jaunts down into the hills south of town or up around "the lake" in Dad's four-door sedan. Along the way Mom called our attention to cows, pigs, horses, or any other animals that happened to be near the road, always adding, "Oh isn't he big"—or "dirty"—or some other remark to attract our attention.

We sometimes took weeklong vacations, intended to be educational, to some spot like the Civil War battlefield at Gettysburg, Pennsylvania, to Washington, D.C., or Niagara Falls. We spent the night in old-fashioned motels that now exist only on side roads or in isolated communities. They were low, one-story buildings that reminded us of elongated ranch houses, with rooms paneled in knotty pine and with vaguely modernist paintings (read cheap prints) bolted to the walls. After several hours in one of these places, we thought that a Howard Johnson's restaurant looked very sophisticated— probably one reason why the chain thrived for so many years along postwar highways.

Our parents' ability to tolerate these weeklong treks must be credited to the strength of paternal love and patience. With two or three kids crammed into the back seat of a car without air conditioning, we set off in August heat as Dad fought traffic on the clogged, two-lane roads that existed nearly everywhere in this day before interstate highways. We soon grew bored with our coloring books and baseball cards and started sniping and slapping at each other. This irritated the old man who reached around, meanwhile trying to keep his eyes on the road, and swung wildly at us with his free arm, inevitably flailing the one child who was innocent. Then he yelled at Mom and demanded, "Do something with these kids."

With the hot muggy air blowing through the windows, at a time when few people had air conditioners in their cars, Mom tried a different tactic: we should all play a game. One of them was "Twenty Questions," a variation on the radio (and television) program of the same name. One of us began by saying, "I am thinking of a place," and the others had 20 questions to zero in on the spot. Another of our car games was counting the different colors of such things as red barns or blue cars. Sometimes we counted farm animals—sheep, cows, hogs, or goats in fields or barnyards by the side of the road. Whoever counted the most things (black cows, red barns, spotted horses, etc.) was the winner. These games were not always successful since we accused each other of counting things that weren't there and argued in Twenty Questions that "question 14" was really "question 13." Another game was "When I go to New York." One of us started by saying, "When I go to New York, I'm going to take a suitcase." The next person repeated this line and added a second article to take to New York, with the third contestant repeating the first two items and adding a third, and so forth. While this seemed to have real possibilities, our short attention spans, shorter memories, and arguments over who was going "to go first" exhausted the game after a few minutes. Mom and Dad sometimes plied us with food and drinks at this point, but that only led to more stops for the bathroom and irritated Dad who just wanted to be done with the day's driving and get home as soon as possible.

We owe our parents a lot for enduring such torture for the sake of family education and togetherness. This endurance was especially true for our dads who chose to spend half of their short, two-week vacations fighting the heat and traffic when they could have been at some cool lake or mountain cottage—or resting at home. Since there were no Disney Worlds or similar theme parks near us, and air travel was beyond most family's budgets at the time, Dad had to bludgeon his 1954 Chevy through downtown Buffalo so we could see Niagara Falls. Such heroics recall a religious advertisement at the time that read, "The family that prays together stays together," a pitch that must have motivated many family vacations. But that a family, which traveled together, could still stay together was something that we appreciated only years later when we set out on family trips with our own wives and children. Of course, many families in our town did not have the means to take even these modest auto excursions, though that was not apparent to us then, since children have the habit of assuming that nearly everyone their age lives the same kind of lives.

Of course, not all activities and subjects were open to the whole family, as when parents insisted that certain topics were not "fit for kids' ears." These forbidden

subjects usually had something to do with sex. Our parents were obviously embarrassed to talk about sex in front of us, and we were just as embarrassed as they were to confront the subject when they were around. Their own hesitations about sex had come from our late Victorian-era grandparents who considered the topic even more unsuitable for decent conversation. Our maternal grandmother, for example, never mentioned the word pregnant when discussing the condition with her female friends but used the code phrase "going to Boston," to describe impending maternity—for reasons that remain a mystery to us. "Martha is going to Boston," or "I hear the Wilson girl is going to Boston," was how she put it. Grandma's modesty also meant that she wouldn't allow her daughters to see her in even the slightest degree of undress. Thus, our moms never saw her except when she was fully clothed and ready for the day, depriving them of even the most accidental glimpse of the adult body.

Family problems were another subject that parents avoided discussing in front of us. This ban also covered parental disagreement that they usually kept bottled up until we were out of the house or in bed. We were equally ignorant of any marital problems among aunts and uncles.

This conspiracy of silence came partly from a sincere desire to protect us from worry and emotional pain. Our parents believed that childhood should be a carefree and happy time, prompting them to say, "You'll have to face all the unpleasant realities of life soon enough." Their refusal to speak of marital problems within the family also came from their firm belief that marriage was a permanent state. For them divorce was a disgrace and a stain on the family's honor. They were later proud to say in the face of escalating divorce rates, "We've never had one in our family, and I hope to God we never will."

When some local couples did get divorced, the whispers could be withering. Based on what we managed to overhear from adult conversations, few splits resulted from a painful but honest decision to end a hopeless union. Instead, the breakup was blamed on sleazy liaisons—affairs with women hidden away in the state capital—or juicy accounts of a woman seen entering a run-down "John Smith" motel with her boss or next-door neighbor. That we had to ferret out these alleged facts, usually by pretending to be lost in play while adults mulled over the details in low tones, made us think the information was all that more scandalous.

It is no wonder we approached the possibility of divorce ourselves with much guilt and hesitation. Six of the sixteen first cousins in our extended family, including the two of us, would undergo this domestic surgery. Because of what our parents had said about divorce, we felt more than apprehensive about what they would say and think. We were both surprised and relieved to find that they loved and supported us just the same. Although they would not countenance divorce for themselves and would continue to shake their heads over the statistics of dissolution, they were wise enough to tolerate a different set of values in a newer generation.

Serious illness was another taboo subject in our homes. Cancer, a painful, wasting, and then mysterious disease, was discussed in the same hushed tones as sex, as if some evil spirit had crept in at night and seized the hapless victim. Our parents talked about heart problems more openly since they seemed less insidious. However, they relegated mental illness to the shadows, expressing sympathy for the victim but thinking such afflictions were incurable.

Our parents similarly shrouded death with mystery and tried to protect us from its sorrows at all costs. Only two or three generations before, our ancestors had accepted death as a normal, if not sad part of family life. They cared for loved ones at home, where they died in their own beds. They then laid the body out in the front room of the house so family and friends could come by and pay their last respects. Children were present to see it all and learned about the reality of death as a part of life. By the time our moms and dads were growing up, the American habit of denying death had begun to take root. During the postwar decades, this denial was especially pervasive. Perhaps this attitude was in reaction to the terrible suffering of World War II, and to the continuing but naïve belief that we Americans might somehow escape the common trials of humanity by shutting out the world with a simple bang of the front-yard gate. It may have been then that euphemisms such as "passed away," or "passed" began to replace the more direct and historically correct, "died." (After all, religious creeds do not read that Jesus "passed away"; nor would we say that famous people like Franklin Roosevelt, Emilia Earhart, or Elvis Presley had passed.)

When our grandparents died, our moms even kept us away from the funeral and the funeral home in the name of childhood innocence. We saw no body, spoke to none of the sympathetic visitors, did not listen to the minister's final words, and did not hear the clods of earth as they hit the casket with a dull thud. The only evidence we had of Grandpa's death was the fact that he was no longer around. In the weeks that followed, our moms stripped away and discarded nearly every vestige of his life: Clothes, papers, books, and the keepsakes of decades went off to the Salvation Army or to the trash heap. Even photographs of Grandpa disappeared into deep storage, almost as if they had to be buried with the person they depicted. It was only months later when we visited the cemetery and heard cheerful stories about him that Grandpa became real again. Our parents' desire to protect us (and themselves) from the agonies of grief was of course sincere, but their conspiracy of silence probably convinced us that death was a far greater terror than it is.

Yet another sensitive subject at home was drinking and alcoholism. Again, the approach was one of avoidance. Our parents never took us into bars or even into restaurants that catered mainly to an adult clientele. Nor did they take us into the liquor store with them, under the assumption that seeing all that booze would somehow undermine our morals and turn us into alcoholics. They themselves were not teetotalers, and they thought it was all right for us to see them have a cocktail at home. There, they thought, alcohol could be consumed in a way that would not shock or demoralize us. The fact that many alcoholics in town were slowly drinking themselves to death at home did not seem to deflect their thinking. Perhaps it was again because they wanted to believe they could shut the front door and leave difficulties outside. As to other addictive drugs, our parents gave little thought to such matters that were so remote from our time and place, save to warn occasionally, "Just one puff or stab of the needle will hook you for life." Most of all, their approach to drug abuse and drinking was one of "staying away." Like sex, they wanted to believe that decent people could simply promise not to go too far and that they would be safe. Consequently, they and many other folks in town looked upon addictions, or supposedly inappropriate sexual activity, as a failure of self-restraint and, as such, a question of personal morality.

Thus, our parents attempted to define what they thought should be the boundaries of our lives. Not surprisingly, this attitude extended to gender roles. They expected the girls to help around the house, while they sent us boys outside to play ball or explore in the woods. Even when there were all boys in the family, we helped with housework only during emergencies. Our community institutions—the churches, schools, scouting organizations, and athletic teams—all reinforced these gender differences. We took it for granted that the little league teams were for boys only. The very thought of a girl trying out for one of the teams was ridiculous.

One motive for this rigid gender definition was fear. Local wisdom held that a boy who didn't join in rough housing would probably grow up to be a sissy or even a homosexual. Curiously, parents expressed little anxiety about tomboy girls—unless it went on too long. The subject of being transgender never came up, even among parents themselves, who could not even imagine the possibility.

The motive for conveying and modeling such role models was supposed preparation for life at a time when most everyone in town agreed, our moms and dads included, that there should be a strict division of labor based on gender differences. They believed, as mentioned earlier, that women should rear the children and manage the household while their husbands went off to work for a living. Mothers had to teach daughters how to cook and clean. Fathers, in turn, had to introduce their sons to competition on the playing field as a way of preparing them for the competition of the workplace, and of life in general. For the same reason, many parents then agreed that it was more important to send a son to college than a daughter.

These gender roles were so pervasive that we took them for granted and were largely unaware of them until we were young adults, and the sexual revolution of the sixties and seventies rejected the whole system. For example, while none of our moms or aunts had college degrees, most of the adult men in our family did go to college, several of them on the postwar "G.I. Bill." None of our moms or aunts worked outside the home until we cousins were well along in school, and even then, they looked for part-time jobs so they could be home when we arrived.

Such part-time positions also reflected our moms' lack of formal job skills and the fact that they were still expected to perform the whole catalogue of household duties in addition to any work outside the home. Another factor was the only partly verbalized anxiety of our dads, who worried that neighbors and relatives might conclude that they couldn't provide for their families and had to put their wives out to work. If this were not enough, both parents, but mothers especially, had to deal with dozens of newspaper and magazine articles that blamed juvenile delinquency on working moms. We often heard them say, "If all those selfish women would just stay home and take care of their kids, none of this would be happening."

Perhaps the most telling incidents of this gender roleplaying appeared around 5:30 in the evening when Dad arrived home from work. He expected to come into a house that was reasonably clean and neat and might comment mildly on some disorganization that caught his attention. Our moms even went so far as to take a bath or shower and change into fresh clothes (always a dress or skirt and never shorts or pants) to greet Dad when he came in the door. After a brief hug and a few words about the day, Mom went off the kitchen to fix dinner while Dad sank slowly into his easy chair, with his drink and the evening paper.

In that short period before dinner—commonly called supper in our part of the country except for special, late evening meals and Sunday dinner after church—the pattern seemed set for life: Dad came home from his trying day and rested with his newspaper and his drink. Mom, whose own exhausting work was not considered as

important as Dad's job and therefore not as tiring, remained
in the kitchen preparing the food that her husband's wages
had earned. We had to evacuate Dad's chair as soon as we
heard his footsteps on the porch and quiet down in his
honor. It is not surprising that some daughters of these
households later joined the Women's Liberation
Movement. Nor is it any mystery to us why so many sons
and daughters of these families ran into serious marital
problems a decade or two later, when these role
expectations were in shambles and neither spouse knew
what was expected in the home.

The mothers in our family, and doubtless in most
local households, tended to see the week as a series of task
days. There was a washing day, an ironing day, a cleaning
day, a grocery-shopping day, and so forth. They also had a
daily round of chores, regardless of the major tasks. These
included making beds, washing and drying dishes three
times a day (by hand and in the kitchen sink), and preparing
all meals, including lunch for us kids and usually our dads,
who in our small town had plenty of time to go home at
noon.

Mom put considerable thought into these meals,
trying hard to make sure we had a balanced diet of meats,

starches, fruits, and vegetables. In those innocent days before anyone talked about cholesterol, sodium, or saturated fats, the main offerings revolved around hefty roasts of beef, pork, and ham, often served up with mashed potatoes smothered in real butter or gravy made from meat juices. She also cooked plenty of steaks, pork chops, and fried chicken, and for dessert, cakes and pies baked with lard. We seldom had fish, probably because in our landlocked part of the country the main source was an unappetizing form of frozen or salted fish. Nor did our mothers, or any other mothers we knew, ever serve lamb, which we considered to be an English dish or affectation of the East Coast.

Although it involved extra effort, Mom usually served the evening meal in the dining room instead of in the large eat-in kitchen. One of her reasons was to make the meal seem more of an official family gathering. She also thought the dining room was a better place to teach table manners. We had to keep our elbows off the table, with our free hand resting in our laps. We were not supposed to have loud conversations or argue at the table. Both parents expected us to eat everything on our plates, for, having grown up during the Depression and then having experienced rationing during the war, they couldn't stand to see us waste food. If we refused to eat a certain dish or to "clean up our plates," they reminded us of "all the poor, starving kids" in China, Korea, India, or wherever else in the world there happened to be a war or famine. In answer to this litany, we sometimes said, "Then send this stuff over there; that's fine with me!"

However troublesome these meals might be, dealing with the laundry for two adults and three children was Mom's greatest chore each week, a task that began on Monday but might drag on until Wednesday or even Thursday. Since she did not own an automatic washer or dryer until later, Mom had to rely on an old, agitator machine. After the clothes had sloshed around long enough, she ran them through a roller-type, squeeze ringer before plunging them into two separate rinse tubs and only then into the waiting laundry basket. In the warmer months, Mom had to carry this heavy load of wet clothes from the basement up to the backyard where she hung them on rope lines strung across the yard and propped up by notched wooden poles. On cold or rainy days, she hung the clothes on lines in the basement. Sometimes sudden showers blew up, sending Mom running outside to yank down the wash before it was soaked. If she didn't make it in time—or if the clothes weren't dry yet—it was back to the basement with the whole load, which she now had to hang on inside racks or lines strung across the basement.

Her ironing began with moistening every piece of clothing from a Coke or Pepsi bottle, filled with water and stoppered with a cork and perforated aluminum cap. To

starch shirts in this era before stay-pressed fabrics, she boiled starch on the stove and dipped the necessary parts of each garment into the slimy mass once it had cooled down. Then she folded every piece and put it away into the proper closets and drawers. It is no wonder the whole ordeal might take her two or three days to complete. Understandably, we were not allowed to change clothes several times a day. And in the absence of stay-pressed fabrics, even the most carefully starched and ironed shirts looked wrinkled by noon.

Mom's cleaning day was generally Friday, in anticipation of the weekend and possible entertaining. She also did spring housecleaning, a major undertaking in our house. It was then that she became ruthless about throwing away our most coveted treasures, from rock collections to pamphlets picked up from auto showrooms or the county fair. She also "rousted" corners, closets, cabinets, cupboards, lampshades, and any other area or item that she might have overlooked on a weekly basis. With Dad's help, rugs went up on the clothesline outside where he beat them magnificently with old wire paddles. Windows were thrown open; storm windows gave way to screen doors; old tires and rusty buckets went out in heaps for the junk man.

Meanwhile the whole house received a complete scrubbing under the theory that this was the best way to rid the house of lingering winter germs. In retrospect, we sense something symbolic and primordial about this annual rite of purification. It was as if we all came together to cleanse ourselves of an evil winter curse and to emerge from hibernation to face the resurrected earth once more.

Much of the motivation for this heroic cleaning each spring came from our old coal furnaces that left a winter's residue of soot and grime on windowsills, curtains, and rugs. The coal itself came from one of the local suppliers, many of whom were in the ice business during the summer. The day the coal men came in their huge, dirty truck was exciting. After backing up to the coal chute, several burly men jumped down and began heaving shovelfuls of shiny black chunks that rattled down into the basement, spattering on the coal bin floor, and bouncing against its wooden sides. The hard anthracite coal from eastern Pennsylvania was the best, but our dads thought it cost too much and settled for the softer bituminous stuff mined in our part of the country. Each winter morning Dad had to go down into a cold basement to empty the ashes from the night before, shake the embers to get the fire going again, and shovel in a new load of coal. Before going to bed, he went down to bank the fire so it would last all night. By morning, the flame was low and the house chilly. It was so cold on many January and February mornings that we found frost on the inside of the windows. Many an early morning, warm buttocks went down on icy cold toilet seats.

Of course, Dad's chores went well beyond superintending the furnace. On Saturdays, there were jobs like fixing leaky faucets or faulty light switches, painting walls and woodwork, or doing minor carpentry work. Almost all the outside jobs fell to Dad, such as shoveling snow, cleaning debris from the gutters and downspouts, mowing the lawn, and raking leaves. When it came to gardening, a gender division again dictated the chores. Dad tended the vegetable garden, which yielded food; Mom presided over the flowers, which provided beauty. The rare exceptions to this rule in our neighborhood were a few men who raised roses as a hobby, but that was supposedly more for botany than for beauty.

Exactly what Dad did when he left the house each morning was hazy to us. We knew plenty of occupations by name—banker, reporter, druggist, and furniture salesman—but since we could not go to work with them, we had little idea of what they did during the day. Once in a while, we went down to the office with Dad on a Saturday morning so he could pick up the mail or retrieve a coat or umbrella left in a fit of absentmindedness. We stood and admired the typewriter, telephone, and large desk, but unlike youngsters a century before, we did not assist a farmer or craftsman father as he did his daily work. Today, few children ever visit their fathers' (or mothers') workplaces, even when closed over a holiday or weekend.

The men of that time had few if any objections to this division of labor based on gender. Nor, as mentioned before, did the women complain, for the most part, about their roles. Yet it appears that many of them adopted a passive-aggressive attitude toward their husbands. In this way, they catered to them outwardly, while getting back at them in ways they could neither prove nor confront. For example, wives would execute a husband's request with silent efficiency and then freeze him out for the rest of the day or week. If that didn't work, they would obliquely criticize their husband to the kids with a comment such as, "Well, don't ask me, it's your dad who ran off to play golf all day." Or, "It's too bad your dad doesn't earn enough money for us to go on a nice vacation like the Murphys took last year."

One consolation for the women was knowing that they would have complete control over the household between the time their husbands left for work and returned in the evening. Often women dreaded their husbands' two-week vacations, which robbed them of their domestic freedom. They might also anticipate their men's retirement with genuine dread, seeing it as a kind of imprisonment instead of many golden years of sharing and togetherness. The retired husband was just as miserable. Having left his job and having never played an important part in the domestic routine, he could feel like a worthless drone around the house, suspecting his wife looked down on him with a mixture of pity and contempt. Trapped in the tight role models of their time and place, it could be very hard for older couples to adjust to living together around the clock. This is yet another area in which the greater gender equality of a later generation has helped both men and women.

Long before any of our parents thought of retirement, our families, like most families, faced several crises, though as with other difficulties, we caught only glimpses of what was happening. One of our dads suffered terrible nightmares and malarial night sweats for years after he returned from war in the Pacific theater. Several marriages in our extended family were strained to the breaking point. At least two parents in the extended family had serious drinking problems, and one father suffered from such severe depression for a while that he had to undergo electric shock treatments at a private sanitarium.

Our parents kept full knowledge of these traumas from us, again on the assumption that we should live carefree lives while growing up. Yet we may have been better off to confront such problems more directly, instead of lying in our beds at night overhearing the nightmarish screams or witnessing a father dissolve into tears as he lost his grip. However, for our moms and dads, who had never heard of family therapy or considered the consequences of a more direct approach, confronting issues in this way was out of the question. Instead, they coped with such crises in the same way they dealt with other problems—confiding to a sister and offering a stiff upper lip to the outside world, trusting that somehow things would get better. The death of a young cousin from Hodgkin's disease brought the larger family closer than any sorrow since the deaths of our grandparents. Still, the adults, including the dead child's parents, dealt with the loss privately. We knew little of their inner agonies then, and an argument could be made that this was for the best, but our own adult trials have suggested that a more open approach, which became more common with the many social and cultural changes a decade or two later, is a better way to confront family crises and grief.

No Overman That Wand
had built churches, or the outskirts where the land was cheaper

5. In God's House

The physical setting of the churches in our town was itself instructive. The established, reformation-era churches all stood in a row along Broad Street in the old part of town. On successive corners, there were St. John's Episcopal, First Presbyterian, and St. Peter's Lutheran. Each inhabited large red brick buildings and had long histories in the community. A block or two out from this center were the Evangelical United Brethren, the Methodists, and the Roman Catholics. The German Reformed and Missouri Synod Lutherans were a little farther out from the core, although still in the older part of town. Smaller sects, often of the fundamentalist variety, had built churches on the outskirts, where the land was cheaper.

It did not take any sociological research for us to know that religious affiliation, like occupation, address, and politics, could be a rough guide to socio-economic status. The principal Methodist Church, for instance, seemed to attract folks such as schoolteachers and merchants of the broad middle class. St. John's Episcopal predictably claimed many of the older, socially prominent families. Among the Presbyterians were many of the local doctors, lawyers, and, most noticeably, the corporate leaders. Factory workers tended to belong to the Methodist Church on the West Side, or to the substantial Catholic community. Of course, the Catholic Church cut across all class lines, as elsewhere, and included managers, professionals, and business proprietors, in addition to blue-collar workers. The biggest religious group in town seemed to be the Lutherans. This was because of the large number of Germans who had settled in the area. Their churches were then prosperous and well supported, but divided by the many splits in the fold, part of a national phenomenon among Lutherans. The small black community had their own AME Church. There was an equally small Jewish congregation, who had converted an old Protestant Church into a synagogue.

Considerable harmony existed among the old-line Protestant congregations, partly because many people by the middle of the twentieth century belonged to a specific church more out of habit and family tradition than because of any strong theological bent. In fact, most churchgoers at the time would have had difficulty explaining what their denomination stood for historically, or exactly what they were supposed to believe. As a result, there were few qualms about church hopping within Protestant ranks, as families took their "letter" and transferred to another congregation in town. Switching churches often happened when someone in a family got angry with the minister over some petty matter. In other cases, the move was for social reasons, with the family believing that membership in a more prestigious church would help them to move up a rung or two on the social ladder. One family we knew began with the Disciples of Christ, skipped to the Methodists, then to the Presbyterians, and finally to the Episcopalians. It seemed to our parents that each move came fast on the heels of a new business success. When a social-climbing family reached the Episcopalians, we assumed they also joined the local country club. In this sense, the churches could reflect the social aspirations that were evident in other aspects of local life.

Many clergymen—and there were no clergywomen in those days in our town—too often labored under an aura of sanctity and seriousness that practically dehumanized them in our eyes. Some, of course, preferred it that way. We noticed that one long-time pastor always wore a black suit, white shirt, and black necktie, and walked around town with a look of sternness mixed with bland benevolence. He almost became another of our town characters as we tried, always unsuccessfully, to imitate his impossible gesture of a grim smile. Over the years, his flock had simply come to know him as "Reverend," ignorant of the fact that they were using this term of address improperly as well as ungrammatically.

We knew another minister who came to town from Philadelphia. Having received an unearned, honorary Doctor of Divinity from an obscure church college, he nevertheless insisted on calling himself "Doctor" Calderwood, the first non-medical doctor that any of us ever heard of. He looked like a tall and spare Anglican vicar (even though he belonged to another denomination), who had stepped straight out of a British movie, with a swag of graying hair falling across his forehead. We noticed that he spoke with a put-on accent, vaguely English. Sometimes he tried to sound more Scottish, especially when he referred to his summer exchange program with a Scottish minister in "Ed'nbruh." He liked to refer to his days at Princeton in sermons, and wore the usual black robe, except that it included three velvet doctoral bars on the sleeves and a colorful doctoral hood flowing down the back, a costume that none of us had ever seen in the pulpit. He intended his sermons to be erudite, and they sometimes were.

Doctor Calderwood sensed our small-town thirst for sophisticated respectability and played it for all it was worth. Local women's groups invited him to speak on his travels, or on the latest books. Executives who belonged to other denominations likewise sought his company, seeing him as a kindred spirit. At his own church, he convinced the congregation of the dubious necessity of erecting a new and largely unneeded building and used his fund-raising skills to obtain the necessary money to build this monument to himself.

Yet as time went on, and Doctor Calderwood experienced the usual disappointments and failures, we grew suspicious of the trappings. His childhood home in New Jersey was, after all, no Buckinghamshire. Nor, as it turned out, had he earned any degrees at Princeton, but had only gone there a few times for brief seminars. We later suspected that his erudition came mainly from perusing old *Reader's Digests*. We also discovered that his Philadelphia was not really Philadelphia, but a minor league suburb where he had served just before showing up in our town. As to the Main Line (a prestigious group of suburbs just west of Philadelphia), which he liked to mention in casual conversation, his only acquaintance was through a car window.

The half-fraudulent Doctor Calderwoods aside, most of the clergy in our town appeared to be decent fellows, if we could break through the dismal image that people heaped upon them. There was a young Presbyterian minister and father of three, whom we often saw out bowling with the men in the church league or taking his family on a picnic. We knew an Episcopalian rector who managed to offset severe looks with a notorious dry wit. Unlike most of the other Protestant clergy, he was not afraid to take a drink or two at a cocktail party, which is one reason we sometimes referred to his denomination as the "Whiskeypalians." We also knew a chaplain at the local reform school as a warm, backslapping man who often spoke at school assemblies and athletic banquets in town.

The pastors of the smaller churches were usually part-time laborers in the vineyard. Most were not well-educated and leaned toward an experiential understanding of faith. We noticed they kept to themselves for the most part and held to a separatist view of religion, believing their own worship and doctrine to be especially blessed by the Lord. These Pentecostal groups met on weeknights, as well as on Sunday mornings. It was exciting to stand outside their open windows on a warm evening and listen to the yelps and moans of men and women in the throes of ecstatic salvation. If we did not understand what was going on inside, we could not deny their enthusiasm.

Yet we would have been wrong to think that pastors alone ran our churches. Much like the ancient Emperors of Japan, they were only the outward manifestations of leadership. The real power in almost every Protestant church in those days seemed to rest in the firm hands of a few dedicated "church women." They may or may not have headed a group in the congregation, such as the Women's Auxiliary or the altar guild. What mattered was their ability to alter congregational opinion—through campaigns among the other women or direct confrontations.

If a new pastor decided there would be two hymns instead of three, he would hear from the women. If he wanted to move the annual Thanksgiving dinner from the Sunday to the Wednesday night preceding it, he had better

seek prior approval from the women, or there would be no one to prepare the meal. If a church board were daft enough to open the church property to a nursery school or to Alcoholics Anonymous, they could expect a telephone call from one or more of the women explaining to them that the designated room had already been set aside every Wednesday morning for their group, and that plans would have to be changed.

There was nothing sinister about these women. Shut out from any official power in the church, they gained positions of influence through steady volunteer work in the choir, the Sunday School, and the church kitchen. Having given more time and energy than anyone else in the congregation, they challenged less dedicated folk to declare their opinions wrong. Two of these women, first cousins named Mae and Fern who were widowed relatively young, belonged to our own Presbyterian fold. Each had given several decades to the church, and they were deadly rivals for influence in the congregation. Their animosity may have begun with an ancient family spite, but it was more likely the result of competition for power and prestige within their second home—the church. We also suspected that these lonely widows had mild crushes on our minister, competing in attempts to flatter and manipulate the hapless man. The icy reception they always gave to his wife seemed to confirm our suspicions.

At potluck suppers in the church basement Mae and Fern each showed up with a favorite dish, keeping an eagle eye on it to see which of the diners snatched it up faster. If some of Mae's chicken casserole was left over, she whisked it off the serving table, toting it around the room and shoving it on innocent parishioners who were already stuffed from a generous sampling of the mountains of food. Not to be outdone, Fern followed in her cousin's wake, peddling her scalloped potatoes among the same groaning guests. Looks of triumph flashed back and forth between the women, as forced compliments issued from the mouths of their trapped victims

Despite such manifestations of pettiness, none of us mistook Mae and Fern for mere lightweights bickering over inconsequential matters. When Fern's husband died, she gathered all her courage and learned to drive a car, reminding anyone who would listen that she had done it to continue her church work. Cousin Mae, for her part, had headed several women's groups in the church. She was a soloist in the choir until an aging voice forced her to step down. Accepting their leadership, the other women in the congregation lined up behind one or the other of them. The minister's wife, already the target of their jealousy, tried to steer clear of both, but she was scorned anyway.

Our minister often tried to make end runs around these women. Yet he was caught two or three times a year over such issues as to whether there should be candles at the Christmas Eve service, as to whether the younger teenagers could serve as helpers in Sunday school classes, or as to whether it had been wise to appoint Mrs. Clark to fill out a term in the missionary society. We can picture these women still, in their flowered hats, jockeying for position like a couple of jealous Hollywood actresses at a cast party, or the co-chairs of a country club dance. Such competition doubtlessly reflected the very limited leadership opportunities for women at the time. Certainly, there was no chance they could become a member of the local clergy, even after our denomination approved of women's ordination in the mid-1950s. The same was true of the other Protestant churches in town, either because their denominations did not sanction women's ordination, or because local congregations like ours would not countenance it. Of course, there was no question of female clergy in the Roman Catholic Church.

Although there were generally good feelings among the denominations in town, many church members assumed their beliefs and worship practices were to various degrees superior to the others—even if they did not fully understand them. We always thought there was something special about fellow Presbyterians. The other denominations maintained similar views, though they were generally not strong enough to prevent church shopping and church climbing among mainline Protestants.

At home, we often heard our parents put special emphasis on fellow Presbyterians. "Oh, he/she belongs to our church," they often observed, indicating that the person was part of a familiar circle. We even associated a particular "look" with members of the different churches in town: we imagined that Lutherans were large and stout; that Episcopalians were long and thin; that Methodists were thin-lipped and bespectacled; and that our own Presbyterians were, as to be expected, tanned, attractive, and smiling. These stereotypes were ridiculous, yet they attested to our need to find mildly tribal peculiarities.

There were a few times when this insistence upon religious identity crossed over the line into downright bigotry, especially in Catholic-Protestant relations in this era before the Vatican II Council. Some adults claimed that Catholics had large families so they could have more voting power and take over the United States through the ballot box. This was the real reason, they added, for the Pope's proclamations against birth control. In our parents' youth, anti-Catholicism blossomed at the annual basketball game between the public and Catholic high schools, a game that was very lopsided because of the much smaller student body at the Catholic school. At one of these matchups during our parents' youth, some public-school students threw a dead fish onto the gym floor (because of the requirement then for Catholics to avoid eating meat on Fridays). The incident brought out the fighting spirit on both sides. Walking back and forth to school, Catholic and Protestant boys sometimes confronted each other with catcalls, which sometimes ended with fists flying.

Some local businesses in our own time refused to hire Catholics, especially the local banks, for reasons that remain a mystery to us, unless it were out-and-out anti-Catholicism. Some equally misguided Catholics continued to insist that all Protestants were damned, that their marriages were invalid, and that their children were technically illegitimate, which did not help matters. In fact, the whole question of intermarriage was a thorny one on both sides. Protestants chafed over the Catholic rule that all children from such unions had to be brought up in their faith, and at the pressure on the non-Catholic spouses to convert to the "one true church." While many of these marriages turned out well, we Protestants believed that the

Catholic hierarchy was taking unfair advantage of young couples whose only error was to fall in love.

Local Catholics, on the other hand, were angry and hurt during the 1960 presidential election, when a bigoted Protestant minister in town launched a series of six anti-Catholic sermons that fall. Afterwards, he had them printed up and circulated them around town as a booklet. They contained the same old propaganda, especially that the Pope would now be ruling the United States under a Catholic president, a charge that had been spewed out during the 1928 campaign against Democratic candidate Al Smith, the first Catholic nominated for the presidency. This local clergyman had simply dusted off the charges and flung them at the Catholic Kennedy. By 1960, however, many Protestants in town felt shame and embarrassment at these accusations.

Most of this animosity came to a sudden halt not long after we cousins had left town, in the era of Pope John XXIII, when the Roman Catholic Church, in the wake of the Vatican II Council, adopted sweeping new conventions that included an emphasis upon ecumenism (a movement toward Christian unity). Almost as if everyone had been waiting for an official signal, the tensions eased all over

America. Local priests and ministers performed joint marriage ceremonies, Catholics visited Protestant churches on special occasions, and families that had been tense over intermarriage felt the atmosphere lifting.

We witnessed very little anti-Semitism in the community, partly because the Jewish community was so small and partly because they contributed far out of proportion to their numbers in civic life. Memories of recent Nazi horrors against Jews also generated local sympathy. Sadly, some residents believed the old and false charges that Jewish merchants were guilty of "sharp" financial practices.

As previously discussed, our own family was Presbyterian. This circumstance had nothing to do with any long-standing tradition, since our maternal grandfather had grown up a Lutheran and our grandmother a Welsh Baptist. Other forebears had been Roman Catholics, Disciples of Christ, and Episcopalians. We traced our Presbyterianism only to the 1920s when our grandfather became enraged— a characteristic of his in all kinds of circumstances—at the Lutheran pastor, and our grandmother enrolled the children in the Presbyterian Sunday school because her next-door neighbor was a Presbyterian and invited the kids to come to their Sunday school. The new church "stuck" and most of the family has been Presbyterian ever since.

Our local Presbyterian congregation had once worshipped in a beautiful Federal-style structure with a tall Christopher-Wren-type steeple and classical columns supporting a pediment with a portico beneath. In the 1890s, it had been replaced with a redbrick, bastard-Romanesque pile, distantly inspired, no doubt, by the then popular designs of architect Henry Hobson Richardson. In our memory, it was a building of unforgiving ugliness, with low wallowing lines and frumpy towers. No one we knew had ever heard of Richardson or his designs, so it was only later that we found a name to give to the mound of mortar and bricks that sheltered our congregation.

This rounded, Romanesque style extended to the interior of the church. To our young eyes, its most impressive feature was a massive dome-like ceiling. Since our parents had told us that the church was God's house, we imagined that He lived somewhere in that large, vaulted space—or maybe up behind the dark green dossal curtain that hung on the chancel wall. In such a room there was surely "no sin that could be hidden and no presence too small for God to see." Only in that sense was the architecture successful.

The worship services themselves seemed interminable to us. The central event in our church, and in most Protestant churches, was the sermon. Everything else appeared to be foreplay. The hymns, the prayers, the coral anthems, and the Bible readings moved along in cadence. Some weeks this routine was broken with the observance of Holy Communion or Baptism. To us Baptism consisted of frightened mothers who turned their infants over to the minister who then sprinkled water on the baby's head. One of our ministers had the unfortunate habit of dousing the screeching child with great scoops of water, and in the process soaking a large part of his black gown. After the Baptism, most mothers took the baby to the nursery and returned to sit beside their husbands. Nevertheless, more than one young mother, undoubtedly proud of her baby, insisted on sitting through the rest of the service with the infant on her lap. Already wide awake from the cascades of holy water, the baby alternately bawled and jabbered through the rest of the proceedings, entertaining just about everyone except the minister. We watched in rib-jabbing fascination as he tried to go on preaching his sermon, sending stern glances toward the offending parents, and sometimes jerking his head briskly to the side in hopes that they would take the hint and leave.

These sermons, long a staple of Protestantism, were supposed to run 20 to 25 minutes in our church, and they nearly always succeeded. Whatever else went on in the service, we knew we would not get out until this dreaded peroration was finished. In earlier years, congregations had looked forward to hearing a well-crafted sermon, but the advent of television, with its brisk and effortless half-hours of entertainment that mixed both sight and sound, made the preacher's task more challenging than ever before. Consequently, our ministers labored mightily to come up with colorful illustrations that might somehow make certain abstract theologies more concrete.

This approach may have worked for the adults, but we kids were left to our own devices. We stared at the stained-glass windows, with their abstract fleur-de-lis and their stylized figures of biblical characters, the meaning of which was totally lost on us. The names below, indicating the persons for whom these great florid windows had been given, shifted our imaginations for a minute. No one appeared to remember who these people were, but we imagined stern, bearded old men and thin-lipped women whose uncompromising piety and personal rectitude had earned them such memorials. It did not occur to us at the time that the departed probably had belonged to a wealthy family which could afford to commission such a memorial window. Hence, a less prosperous but more upright member of the congregation could not look forward to this posthumous honor. In this sense, social class followed one into the afterlife, even if that afterlife existed only in stained glass.

After tiring of the windows, we turned to the small yellow pencils in the pew racks, using them to scribble on the service bulletins or the offering envelopes placed there for visitors. Having exhausted our doodles, we began counting the number of panes in the huge overhead chandelier, or the lighted glass panels in the arch over the chancel area. There were 13 of them.

Such diversions might bring us to the middle of the sermon, which was about the place where the minister was launching into point two of this three-point sermon—unless, of course, a fourth and even a fifth point came to mind as he was closing. These addenda were like a Beethoven symphony, with one climax after another, followed by two or three endings. Long before this time, the minister's drone threatened to put us to sleep, unless we tried some other way of surviving, which was watching the preacher's gestures. Sometimes he ran his hands around the side of the pulpit; at other times, he emphasized a point by gazing at the ceiling as if appealing to the Lord. One of our ministers tried to look thoughtful by closing his eyes and pinching the bridge of his nose. While our clergymen were certainly not fist pounders, they sometimes drove home a message by slapping the side of the pulpit with an open hand, a gesture that caused more than one bobbing head to snap to attention. In the last analysis, we discovered that sermons are like jokes—hard to remember. Yet we still laugh and remember the laughter. Perhaps we absorbed a lot more from these childhood sermons than we remember; perhaps they became more a part of us than we know.

If we found the sermon a dreaded prospect, the choir could be very entertaining—not so much for the music as for the expressions of the singers, who were corporate executives, prominent attorneys, the parents of our friends, or even our own moms and dads. We looked for the eyebrows to bounce up on the high notes, and for the odd rounding of the mouths as they formed the long

"Os." We took perverse pleasure when a straining tenor seemed to shout more than sing, or when a bass, groping for an especially low note, dug his chin into his breastbone. Such gestures were, of course, not the point of their performance, but no one could have convinced us back then.

Nor did we appreciate the fact that churches have been the great repository and guardian of much of our musical heritage in the West. Other than school, church was the only place any of us sang or heard good music. The large pipe organ in our church was one of the best in the region, and it boomed out Bach fugues during the prelude so loudly that the windows rattled. The organist toned down the volume a little during the hymns, but she clearly enjoyed the power of the instrument. The men in our congregation probably did not mind this, since most of them just mouthed the words anyway. Some of them, perhaps because they thought singing was effeminate or because they were too self-conscious, never even bothered to open the hymnal. Our congregational singing was thus carried by the female voices. There were always two or three women, who imagined themselves operatic contraltos, causing them to trill and screech without shame.

We also noticed that most adults had a hard time keeping a straight face during these moments of virtuosity, but we sniggered unrestrained, to the wrathful stares of our parents.

In fact, the heaviness of our worship services set us up for such sniggering. Any variation from their sober and somber tone delighted us. When we came to the weekly Psalter, a responsive reading of biblical psalms in which the minister pronounced one line and the congregation the next, we listened for the poor soul who got caught up in the activity and continued to read on into the minister's lines, and then sat red-faced when he realized that everyone else was silent. Such bloopers were especially satisfying when committed by a bank president or the fur-coated wife of a prominent business leader.

Since we did not grasp much of what went on around us on a Sunday morning, it was thus the sights, smells, and sounds of church that captivated us. As Protestants, these elements were not built into our services as they were into the Roman Catholic masses, with their candles, incense, bells, and colorful vestments. Yet even in our church, they were unintentional presences. Besides the architectural and decorative features of the church, there was the musty odor of old hymnals and last week's flowers. These mingled with a hint of pew varnish, this week's flowers, women's perfumes, and men's colognes. Catching our eyes were the women in their best dresses, including white gloves and a riot of colorful hats such as no one has seen since. One of our aunts even contended that she sat in the back pew so she could admire the hats, though the real reason may have been that she was usually late for church. Men, by contrast, wore the same conservative business suits that we saw them wearing downtown.

We also had to dress up for church, the only chance we had in those younger years to wear something approximating a suit. We trimmed it off with carefully shined leather shoes, a clip-on bow tie, and sometimes a pork-pie hat just like the one Dad wore. The girls underwent a similar transformation, donning pretty dresses over stiff crinolines, little white gloves, straw hats, thin white ankle socks, and black patent-leather shoes. This dressing up made us feel important. Our clothes were also an essential ingredient in the "Sunday mood" of cleanliness, order, and, our parents hoped, of self-restraint.

Another lesson we learned in church was patience and the ability to cope with boredom. There we were tested weekly, knowing our parents were up in the choir loft keeping track. No wonder we greeted the final hymn and benediction with a tremendous feeling of relief. The next obstacle was getting out of church. The adults crept slowly into the center aisle and then stopped to visit with each another. Once out of our pew and up the aisle we hit another blockade at the line to greet the minister, who stood in the narthex shaking hands. Slowly, agonizingly slowly, they moved. There was no good escape from this trap. If our bladders were about to burst, and they often were by then, we cut our way through the staggering herds, bypassed the minister, and charged down the steps to the men's room, brazenly ignoring the "harrumphs" from the jostled adults.

It is difficult to say what we learned—what lessons have remained from these bumblebee mornings of drowsy tedium. In our catechism the first question was, "What is the chief end of man?" The correct answer, we learned, was "To worship God and enjoy him forever." More than once, we thought a better answer would be "To worship God and ENDURE him forever."

Still, through the haze of boredom, there came a few simple but powerful ideas. One was to try very hard to be good people and to help one another. Another held that Jesus was a special person, and that we should believe in him to overcome the finitude of this life. There was also the idea of an invisible law that neither parents nor police enforced, but God himself, who kept a watchful eye on each of us. Finally, there was no escaping a note of fatalism, the result, perhaps, of our Calvinist/Presbyterian heritage. Since God was the sovereign of the universe, there was nothing we could do but accept life as it came. It was a species of kismet set in our American town. Thus, we often heard adults in our family say, "When your time comes, it comes. This *was* to be, and we'll just have to live with it."

In addition to these deterministic concepts, we were led to believe that there was a close connection between religion and patriotism. A large American flag stood to the right of the lectern in the church, and we often heard the minister associate God with the American way of life. In the minister's mind—and in the minds of most in the congregation—there was no question that God was on "our side." This notion was probably a carryover from the Puritans' belief that Massachusetts, and later all of America, was a New Israel, and its citizens were a new

Chosen People. Our recent and successful crusade against the evils of Nazi and Japanese imperialism reinforced our sense of being a chosen people. In the 1950s, this naive self-confidence took on a new life as the Korean War and the growing dread of international Communism gave us Christians another righteous cause. Ministers, teachers, and politicians almost always introduced the word Communism with the adjective "godless" or "atheistic." We sincerely prayed for the boys in Korea, and that our own fathers and uncles would not have to go back into the service. Mostly we prayed for the defeat of this worldwide monster—or even better, that God would perform a miracle and bring the Reds to receive Christ as the true "light of the world."

This blending of national purpose with religious faith was sincere for the most part, even if it was naive. Unfortunately, scoundrels, then and later, used it to justify an unquestioning acceptance of American foreign policy. However, in church, it somehow seemed right that we should cast the world into the forces of light and darkness and believe that God would stand up with "His own" on the day of battle. As we belted out that old Victorian hymn, "Onward Christian Soldiers," few of us doubted that we were singing about past crusades, as well as about the battles to come.

This view of the world was our own version of "American Exceptionalism." That America was exceptional, with its freedom and prosperity, we did not doubt. However, the belief that God favored the American people above all others was arrogant as well as dangerous and helps to explain the sense of ill-conceived mission that was already preparing the ground for the fiasco in Vietnam.

Our church was certainly not exceptional in its all-white congregation, a fact of religious life that we shared with all the other congregations in town. This racial segregation was not official, but we wonder what the reaction would have been if a black family had entered our midst one Sunday morning. We suspect that members of the congregation would have ignored them, but such an event was very unlikely, since any Black family in town would have known that they would not be welcome. Nor was it likely that an Asian or Latino family would have come through the church doors, since, as referenced earlier, we do not recall that anyone hailing from those parts of the world lived in our town. This circumstance was truly unfortunate since we were deprived of finding a sense of common humanity through worship. Looking back, it was our own lived experience of what the Reverend Dr. Martin Luther King Jr. would later say—that "The most segregated hour of Christian America is eleven o'clock on Sunday morning."

Sunday school was a very different experience from church. It was less tedious, with lessons geared to our level of understanding. There were plenty of kids to play with, and many of our teachers were young mothers or elementary school teachers we already knew.

Sunday school began with "assembly time," when all the students, teachers, and administrators met in the big assembly room. The superintendent, a young father himself, called the roll and took up the collection. He made announcements and handed out our Sunday school attendance pins. These were tangible rewards for perfect or, at least, regular attendance. The first-year pin was a small, round brass badge covered with glazed-on enamel that featured a cross and other Christian symbols. If we remained faithful for a second year, we received a brass wreath that encircled the first pin. Thereafter the reward was little bars, which we could attach to the bottom of the pin and wreath, with the words "third", "fourth", "fifth," and so on written across them. After a few years, the most loyal pupils could display a lapel full of Christian medals, not unlike the soldiers who had gone to war and returned to town with a uniform covered with battle ribbons. Some kids were so proud of their Sunday school awards that they wore them to school during the week. If we look closely, we can still see these attendance pins in flea markets across the state. Some of us can still find them lodged in the recesses of a sock drawer.

It was also during assembly time that we sang Sunday School songs, rousing counterparts of the more somber hymns that we heard in church or songs written specifically for Children. Among the old standbys were "Jesus Loves Me," "The B-I-B-L-E"—and, of course, "Onward Christian Soldiers," to which we sometimes stomped around the big Sunday school room as Miss Wilson banged out the tune on an old upright piano.

Our Sunday school teachers could be very interesting to watch. One female teacher wore a peaked felt hat with a large feather. She also had the habit of taking a flowered handkerchief from between her breasts and wiping her eyes or nose with it. We thought she must have been overcome by some moving part of the lesson, only to discover years later that she suffered from allergies. A male teacher was famous for picking his nose and rolling the product between his thumb and forefinger before dropping in onto the floor. Sometimes the newly mined treasure was a little wetter than expected and we watched in fascination as he tried surreptitiously to flick it off his fingers.

One of our favorite Sunday school teachers, Miss Dorothy Campbell, is remembered by generations of youngsters. Miss Campbell was a late middle-aged woman

at the time. She had graduated from normal school (an earlier name for teachers' colleges) and became a second-grade teacher in our town, where she stayed for the next 40 years. As a religious woman, she volunteered to teach Sunday school and stayed long after she had retired from her public-school classroom. Every Sunday morning, she was there with her flannel board, which she used to illustrate the better-known Bible stories. She threatened to quit each spring but had no more intention of leaving than a little boy who threatens to run away from home. We knew she enjoyed being begged to stay on and was flattered to think she was indispensable to the program. We also knew that she would be back in the fall to greet a new batch of second graders. There would be another year of cutout crosses, pumpkins, Easter lilies, and praying hands to pin on the walls, and of prodigal sons to return home from behind the flannel board.

Miss Campbell never married and increasingly came to seem like the dedicated, virginal mother, a sort of unofficial Protestant nun. Only now do we realize that what she really wanted was to play the part of a child. At Christmas and Easter, she was completely childlike. She even slipped in front of the adults, falling into the singsong voice that we all associate with small children. In class, she delighted in the same things that pleased us. As we grew older her style seemed cloying, but not to her continuing stream of second graders. The world of adults became less and less palatable for her, less worth living in. In the end, she became a curiosity of sorts—tall, angular, and graying, but still pretty in her teacher's frocks. She was an adult who had retreated into the world of innocents.

What we learned from her, and the other Sunday school teachers is as difficult to define as what we gained from the first years in school. At school, we learned to read, add, spell, and draw. However, we spent 30 hours a week in school, and only one hour at Sunday school. Yet we came away with a vague outline of Jesus's life, an imperfect memorization of the Ten Commandments, and a rich collection of Bible stories. There was David fighting off the great Goliath with only a sling and a rock, an account that stirred our sense of bravery. The story of Adam and Eve in the garden, enticed by the wicked serpent to eat of the forbidden fruit, portrayed the temptations that we all faced in life. (Of course, our teachers never breathed a hint of the sexual connotations in this famous story.) We also heard about "smarty" little Joseph, dressed in his colorful coat, and mocking his brothers, all of which reminded us of the more spoiled kids on the playground or in the neighborhood. The story of the mighty Samson, undone by a clever woman and her scissors, left us with knowledge of our own inner weaknesses, and with some reinforcement of prejudicial suspicions about the alleged wiles of the female sex. We often confused the story of Jonah in the belly of a whale (actually a big fish) with a similar episode in Walt Disney's cartoon version of Pinocchio, which misses the point entirely.

Then there were all the New Testament stories and parables that we might apply to our daily lives. These included Little Zaccheus in his tree, Jesus's walking on the water, the Good Samaritan's helping the victim of thieves, and the Prodigal Son's return to the arms of a forgiving father. There was also the great drama of Jesus's final days as he moved from the glory of Palm Sunday to the sorrow of the Last Supper and the Crucifixion and finally to the miraculous resurrection of Easter morning. Devices such as movies, filmstrips, and Miss Campbell's flannel board helped us to visualize these stories, but the best were the clever cartoons that some of the teachers used as illustrations. Still, such aids failed when they tried to explain abstract teachings such as the Ten Commandments. One filmstrip's description of the famous Seventh Commandment--"Thou shalt not commit adultery"—was especially confusing. It showed two men walking down a dusty road holding hands with one woman. The next frame projected a large "X" on the entwined hands of the woman and one of the two men, all of which left us with the impression that adultery meant "adulthood," and that such a life must be very dull.

The Bible story that remained the most vivid, perhaps because it so happily fit the preconceived ideals of most people in town was the "Parable of the Talents." In it, Jesus speaks about a master who goes on a trip and leaves the responsibility for his affairs in the hands of three servants. He gives each of them a sum of money known as "talents." When he returns, he calls for an accounting and discovers that the first two have invested the funds and have turned a profit. The third servant, frightened at the possibility of losing his investment, has buried his talents in the ground. The disgusted master soundly scolds and punishes this timid man for his lack of imagination and courage. In the somewhat Calvinistic setting of our Presbyterian Church, we took this parable to mean that there is no substitute for hard work, and that God has given each of us talents that we should "invest" without fear of the consequences. Laziness and lack of industry, we believed, were not just personal flaws but serious shortcomings in the eyes of God. (We might have asked, "If this were the same God who predestined everything how could those who did not use their talents be blamed for failing?" Of course, neither we nor our Sunday school teachers would have brought up or even recognized this contradiction.)

In this way, we were presented with the famed Protestant work ethic, as people understood it in our time and place. Such a hard-core, faith-bound belief could explain why so many residents had utter contempt for social welfare programs. According to them, people who were poor or who did not work were not only lazy but also immoral. To their way of thinking, work—hard work— was part of the divine plan. Those who refused to "put their shoulders to the plow" did not deserve a free ride at the taxpayer's expense. If too many people got away with such chiseling, God's plan and the entire American way of life would tumble like the walls of Jericho.

We accordingly admired needy persons who refused to go on welfare. One case concerned a Mrs. Bowers, the recent widow of a smalltime farmer and mechanic who dropped dead suddenly, leaving her with two teenage boys and little money. No matter how hard things were, Mrs. Bowers could not imagine turning "to welfare." Neighbors, friends, and church members all pitched in to help support the family until she could find work. Even after she did get a job, people continued to remember her with special gifts—a sack of potatoes left on the porch, two freshly killed and skinned rabbits dropped at her door by hunters, or maybe a barely worn winter jacket that was just the right size for a son. The gifts were anonymous since no one wanted to undermine the family's pride. In most people's minds, the Bowerses were different from other poor families, admired as hard workers and proud people who refused to disgrace themselves by going to the county welfare office. They were fortunate in having a network of friends and neighbors who could afford to be generous. Many other needy people in town were not so lucky.

Ironically, another individual who escaped the stigma of welfare was Howard Ross, the only son of a prominent local family. Howard had grown up in the early part of the twentieth century as a pampered and protected boy. When his parents died and the family fortune faded with them, Howard was completely unprepared to work and earn his own living. Locals who remembered his parents found ways to help the spoiled son. He would sit down at a drugstore lunch counter and order a cup of coffee. The druggist's wife quietly made him a sandwich and served it to him free of charge. Before long, the drugstore visits became a daily habit for Howard. Members of another prominent family, who fondly recalled his parents, always invited Howard to their annual Christmas party. They asked him to come by early enough to take a bath and change into one of his host's suits, carefully laid out on the bed in the guest room. They considered Howard to be "one of their own" and did whatever they could to help him avoid the disgrace of county assistance.

Sympathy for Howard's plight was thus an exception to the contempt which more fortunate residents heaped on people who did not (or could not) work, perhaps because adults accepted the argument that his parents' pampering had ruined the poor soul and made him one of the deserving poor. In other words, coming from a "good family" somehow made a person worthier of sympathy and help. For the most part, however, our elders believed that nothing good comes without toil and suffering.

The corollary to this argument was that the easy life only breeds unhappiness and tragedy. If we came across a spoiled child, our parents shook their heads and clucked, "That boy is going to face a really hard life as soon as he leaves his mother's apron strings. Other boys will probably beat him to a pulp!" Similarly, when we asked why we couldn't join the local country club, our parents answered that many of its members went into debt just to pay their dues. They knowingly added, "Every month when the country club bills come out, they're lining up at the bank and taking out loans." The good life, they insisted, was full of sacrifice and hard work that had nothing to do with the "artificial lives" of country club phonies. After all, Jesus had not saved humanity by doling out chocolate cream puffs, but by his painful death on the cross. In many ways, this message was valid and sincere, but it was easily twisted, causing us to feel needlessly guilty when our own families became more prosperous in the years ahead and some joined country clubs.

This belief that hard work, and at least some suffering, were good for us may have been behind the reluctance of adults in our family to praise any of us too lavishly for what we had accomplished. We could usually tell they were proud of us, but we think now that they held back from saying just how proud there were for fear that we might think too well of ourselves and conclude that life would always be easy.

Beyond such religious messages, many of them contorted by our limited view of the world, the Bible did offer a wider view of life. It became a book of stories, strange visions, and pungent quotations, which took us beyond the range of our normal existence. This exotic quality could arouse a sense of something more, of a world beyond our limited lives in a small town.

Fortunately, church was more than worship services and Sunday school classes. There was a spate of social events connecting us to the church community. Among our favorites were suppers in the large church basement. Preparation for the more ambitious meals could take all day, with half a dozen women showing up in the morning to cook, set tables, and swap church gossip. Sometimes the men took their turn in the kitchen, baking the Thanksgiving turkey or a ham. It was an odd but not uncomfortable sight to see our fathers and other familiar men in aprons and chefs' hats playing the parts that we usually associated with women. It was an exception that proved the rule.

Families arrived around six in the evening for these feasts. They sat at long tables, which were collapsible for easy storage but still hideously heavy. On each table, we found a homemade centerpiece fitting for the occasion. Around Thanksgiving, it was a small turkey made from an apple for the body, raisins for the eyes, and toothpicks for the legs. Other times there were sprays of autumn leaves or artificial snowballs, put together by a group of women who volunteered for the task. More common and more popular than the 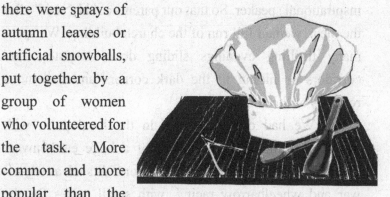 prepared dinners at church were the "potluck" suppers to which each family brought its own table service and a covered dish to share with the others. We were always amazed at how 50 to 75 families could show up and find that the balance among meats, vegetables, and desserts was just right. Surely, some might think, this was evidence of a divine hand or maybe a modern-day version of Jesus feeding of the multitude.

While a few of these suppers were connected to a specific event, such as Thanksgiving or a fund-raising effort, most of the time they came out of a simple desire to "get together." Often there was some sort of entertainment, such as a male quartet from the choir, a magician, or an inspirational speaker. So that our parents could "visit" after the meal, we had full run of the church building. We spent many thrilling evenings sliding down banisters and corridors or hiding in the dark corners and cavernous recesses of the church.

We had church picnics in the local park, with gallons of lemonade ladled out of a huge earthenware crock. There were organized games for kids such as tug-of-war and wheelbarrow racing, with small prizes for the winners. Meanwhile, our parents sat in the evening breeze and talked. Here, too, the potluck style resulted in that unplanned balance of homemade dishes. Other outdoor events included hikes through the woods or visits to a church camp in the southern part of the state. In the cooler months, there were the father-and-son and mother-and-daughter banquets and brisk walks through the central part of town to sing Christmas carols.

In addition to these all-member outings, there were church groups that met on a regular basis. These were contrived to appeal to every interest imaginable—according to age, marital status, and even doctrinal stance. There were women's discussion groups, sewing circles, a young couple's club, an older folk's group ("senior citizen" being a euphemism that we never heard until years later), a men's Bible class, youth groups according to age, a poetry contingent, and, of course, the choirs, one for adults and one for children and youth. Many of the adult groups were segregated by gender, with the belief that men and women thought differently and therefore would enjoy different activities.

Church offered us some valuable lesson for life, as well as an array of fun activities for children and youth. However, the overall religious culture and view of the world left little space for social criticism or advocacy of change.

6. School Days

All our elementary teachers were women, many of them unmarried. Several were sisters who had remained in their parents' homes and lived in modest comfort. Like Miss Campbell at Sunday school, they seemed very much like nuns who had taken vows of poverty, chastity, and obedience: chastity in that they did not marry or, presumably, enjoy sex of any kind; poverty in that they received skimpy wages for a lifetime of commitment; and obedience in that they were true soldiers of a community social policy and carried out school board regulations without question. With rare exceptions, school teaching was one of the few professions open to them before the women's movement.

Still, they could wield tremendous influence over us—and the hundreds of other kids who had sat in their captive audiences.

Community demands on teachers weren't limited to the unmarried ones, since school authorities demanded high standards of conduct from the entire faculty. A teacher had to leave her job at the first signs of pregnancy, presumably because the condition would compromise the teacher's moral position or cause students to ask why her belly was swelling. In our day, teachers still had to behave like Methodist preachers, forbidden to smoke in public or to go into bars or cocktail lounges. Even their clothes reflected such expectations. They wore low-heeled shoes and dresses, or at least skirts and blouses. This official "costume" was a hardship for educators who earned such low salaries. It was also an uncomfortable and inefficient type of dress for elementary-school teachers who did a lot of standing, walking, and bending over, not to mention having to cope with paint, paste, and clouds of chalk dust.

Townspeople saw teachers as a breed apart. Their pay was low, in part because of stingy taxpayers but also because people in the community assumed that educators were members of a semi-religious calling. "Teachers should be dedicated," adults often remarked when there was a question of raising taxes for better salaries. Since teachers' lives were supposed to be above reproach, we couldn't imagine them in any other role. We had a hard time picturing them with lives outside the classroom and could hardly imagine, even in high school, that married teachers might enjoy sex with their spouses.

Although there were some cross or incompetent teachers in our elementary school, most of them genuinely cared about our intellectual, social, and emotional development. One primary teacher named Miss Benson went far beyond the call of duty, often spending part of a small salary to buy an impoverished student a new dress or pair of shoes, always making sure that other pupils knew nothing about it. Miss Benson also spent many Saturday afternoons taking an underprivileged kid to the county fair, or on some other outing that the parents could not afford. She also put in long hours after school drilling students with learning difficulties in the intricacies of long division and other tricky subjects.

Very well intentioned, but also misguided, was Mrs. Hart. We remember that one of her struggling students was unfortunate enough to have both a brother and sister who were just a few years older and were straight-A students. Mrs. Hart often compared him to these academically more talented siblings by saying, "Why can't you be more like your brother Ricky or your sister Nancy." She probably meant to encourage him, as if to say, "Since your brother and sister did so well, then *so can you*," but her words only discouraged and humiliated him.

Then there was Mrs. Kramer who could blow her stack at any moment. Once, when a student was banging on an old upright piano, she crept up behind him, pounded him on the back, and pulled him over onto the floor, piano bench and all, shouting, "Stephen you're a disgrace to yourself and your whole family." As far as we know, she was never called on the carpet. A generation later, the parents would have sued her and the school for child abuse.

Our elementary school was a handsome red brick structure. It was built in 1917 in a vague Colonial Revival style, a design that many school systems used in the early twentieth century, partly as a way of teaching patriotism and respect for our colonial ancestors. The building was three-stories high and intended to house about 600 students, ranging from the first through the eighth grades. Inside were polished wooden floors that snapped and crackled as we walked. Enlivening otherwise ugly, light green classroom walls were large, framed prints featuring patriotic scenes from the American past, such as the Pilgrims landing at Plymouth Rock or Washington crossing an ice-filled Delaware River. Seen every year for eight years, they took on heroic dimensions: the simple picture of a Puritan father pointing off toward the woods as his wife trudged along in the snow behind him began to resemble some unspoken drama acted out before our eyes. In the hall near one of the first-grade rooms, there was a cheap, lithograph copy of Gilbert Stuart's famous unfinished portrait of George Washington. Beneath Washington's head and shoulders was a fuzzy white area—the unfinished part—that looked very much like billowy clouds. It seemed to show the Father of Our Country on his own cloud up in Heaven. Beside him was a framed print of first lady Martha Washington, very much finished and looking part of this earth.

The school also had certain unmistakable odors, a combination of floor wax, chalk dust, pencil shavings, school paste, and (on the first day of school particularly) of stiff, new blue jeans. Yet even before confronting such sights and smells, we had to learn a very important fact about our playground: it was sexually segregated. There was never any official explanation for this rule; nor did we know how long it had been enforced. Some of us thought it was because the boys were rougher than the girls were. We later guessed it had something to do with sexual morality, in case boys and girls got too familiar with each other in the wrong ways. Whatever the explanation, the rule reinforced the belief that boys and girls were very different and probably unequal. In any case, a long central sidewalk split the playground area, with the "boys' side" to the left and the "girls' side" to the right. Even if a ball "accidently" bounced across the sidewalk, we knew it was better to ask permission before running over to get it. There was always the alternative of yelling across and asking some girl to throw it back. This worked unless the girl, itching to see a boy break the rules, yelled back tauntingly, "Come and get it yourself!"

Our principal, Mr. Biederman, took this segregated playground rule with great seriousness. At the time, he was a stocky man of medium height in his late fifties, with steel-rimmed glasses, a pale face, and a round balding head of graying hair. Behind his back, we dropped the obligatory "Mr." and referred to him as just Biederman, or often as

"Old Biederman." We remember him best as he stood by the window of his second-floor office watching to see if anyone crossed over the great playground divide. The shouts and general turmoil of the schoolyard came to an immediate halt whenever we saw him at the window. All eyes gazed upward as Biederman pointed to the miscreant. The crowds parted, leaving the offender alone in the center of a wide circle. Paralyzed and staring at the dreaded window, the accused watched as Biederman's finger, curled like that of a Persian satrap, motioned him to come forward and present himself at the office. Whispers began to circulate through the clumps of students as the doomed child's name made the rounds. In time, the young perpetrator returned to his classroom, red-faced and sheepish, while we all stared at him—and it always was a "him"—with a mixture of sorrow and awe for the terrors he must have endured and at the fact that he could still stand.

A dread summons to Biederman's office could come at any time and for any number of infractions, crossing over to the girls' side being only one of them. Running to or from school, pushing in line, throwing stones or snowballs, and, of course, talking back to the teacher

could all result in a visit to the principal. The punishment
for breaking any of the rules, we heard from older students,
was Biederman's electric paddle. Just what this paddle was
like, nobody knew for sure. Some thought it connected to
an electric motor that propelled it against the victim's rear
end with terrible speed and force, while others believed that
it was equipped with electric spikes that added a horrible
shock to the already painful whipping. Some believed that
Biederman owned a series of paddles hanging behind the
door, each with its own gruesome specialty: one had holes
drilled in it to facilitate the swiftness of the stroke; another
was cut narrowly for better accuracy; a third was made of
metal and could be heated up for a hot whipping.

One of our cousins made a couple of trips to that
dreaded place, where many claimed to have heard such
hideous screams behind a heavy, closed door. Among the
sins committed were throwing snowballs (and afterwards
hitting a particularly obnoxious kid who told an older sister
about it) and hurling a smaller classmate against a pile of
"rag bags" that the whole school had collected in an early
recycling project that would somehow benefit poor people.
As a two-time visitor, he could attest that although
Biederman casually moved toward the door as if to grab

something from behind it, nothing worse than a good, long scolding followed. Yet we all liked to think that such tortures were real, for like our half-hearted beliefs in spooks and monsters abroad in the night, these stories of hideous punishments at school were exciting to imagine and relate.

Our principal was clearly not as bad as the students thought, or that we sometimes remember in the retelling. However, he did in truth spank kids, always without parental consent and without consultation with higher authorities. His judgment alone was enough. Principal, teachers, and parents simply believed that teaching children discipline was one of the school's missions. If we did not learn to obey, they said, we could never hold down a job or lead others. The fact that our parents had once gone to school under the same principal probably contributed to their support for his rigorous discipline.

Corporal punishment or the fear of it was only one way of keeping us in line. Another was a daily diet of regimentation. When the first bell rang in the morning, we had to make two parallel lines outside the door, one line for the boys and a separate one for the girls. At the sound of the second bell, we marched into the school, completely silent and keeping "our hands to ourselves." The drill was repeated during recess and at lunchtime. Of course, the teachers supervised this lining up and marching from one place to another, pulling violators out of line for a scolding or sending them to Biederman's office. During our parents' school days, there was some ritual to the process. Back then, everyone marched up the building's central steps each morning and saluted the American flag, as an old Victrola set up on the stair landing ground out some patriotic march such as "Stars and Stripes Forever." Yet another example of regimentation was the unison responses we gave to the teachers each morning in return for their greetings: "Good morning boys and girls," to which we all replied, "Good morning, Miss…"

There was a special emphasis on tardiness. The authorities viewed lateness as a serious infraction of the rules and saw it as a bad reflection on both the students and their parents. People who could not show up on time, teachers insisted, were not dependable, and tardiness in later life could cost us our jobs. They viewed our failure to return a report card or permission slip on time as another sign of poor character.

The greatest terror of any kid at school was that he might not be able to control his bodily functions. Wetting one's pants—or worse, dirtying them—was all too common in the lower grades. The overheated classrooms soon brought out the rich aroma of these accidents, causing generally sympathetic teachers to go to the unfortunate child and send him to the bathroom to clean himself up. But the embarrassment had just begun, since he now had to face the rest of the class with a big damp spot (or worse) in the middle of his pants. Years later, one classmate could still feel the acidic sting of pee-stained, frozen blue jeans that clung to his legs during a winter recess and the long walk home.

Getting sick at school could be just as terrifying. Two or three times every year, we heard that curious glottal sound of a doomed kid vomiting all over the desk and floor. Heads turned toward the involuntary sufferer as the sticky pink and orange fluid began to congeal on books and papers. Our teachers again understood, but Mr. Dobbins the janitor, who had to come in and clean up the mess, surely was not. Mr. Dobbins was a World War I veteran and had been the janitor at school for years. Surprisingly fit for his age, he nevertheless looked like he had just stepped out of the trenches. He shaved about once a week and his steel gray hair looked stiff as barbed wire. He wore a putrid shade of tannish-yellow work clothes that gave off a musty, metallic odor. He took it upon himself to maintain discipline whenever he saw students acting up in the halls, barking out orders as if he were still a drill sergeant.

Mr. Dobbins always took his time answering the vomit calls. In he came, shuffling and muttering evil thoughts under his breath as he slammed his mop, bucket, and broom down on the floor. Everything now stopped while we watched in fascination as he sprinkled some disinfected sawdust over the mess and swept it up. Once Mr. Dobbins was so angry that he banged shut a vomit-filled book, spattering everyone within several feet and planting the seeds of future vomit calls. Then turning to our teacher, who was almost as scared of him as we were, he croaked, "You might as well take this thing out and burn it." The disinfectant smell lingered for the rest of the day.

Despite our school's dedication to study and regimentation, there were curious periods when all was held in suspension. Every early October the principal allowed us to listen to the World Series, then played in the afternoon, over the radio through the school's public address system. Even in years when none of the nearby teams had made it, the play-by-play buzzed across the classroom as we drew pictures, copied spelling words, or otherwise spent the afternoon free from regular schoolwork. Twice in 1953 we were sent home to watch important events on television—there being no TVs in the school—first for the inauguration of President Eisenhower and then for the coronation of Queen Elizabeth II. Most of us volunteered to take a bus student home so he would not miss seeing these monumental events. There were also those warm and still Friday afternoons when the first or second grade teachers took us out to the high-school football field, which was located just behind our elementary school. We plopped down on the bleachers together, listened to the band practice for the big game that night, and felt very warm and special as we sat there with our teachers.

Every spring the Duncan yo-yo people sent three yo-yo experts to our playground to amaze the kids with their tricks and, of course, in hopes that we'd run out and buy their wares. The demonstrators were invariably Filipinos, the men in loose-fitting Hawaiian shirts and the women in skimpy skirts and blouses that lured even the smallest boys. They would "walk the dog" "go around the world," and perform other feats of yo-yo virtuosity. Some of us did make a "bee-line" after school to one of the three small stores near the school grounds where we spent several week's allowance on a spinner yo-yo. The most expensive and coveted models had three or four pieces of cheap cut glass imbedded into the wood on either side.

These stores near the school also sold a variety of candies. The favorites were root beer barrels, miniature Reese's Cups, and red or black licorice whips. They also stocked black licorice in the shape of infant children that many thoughtlessly—or maybe not so thoughtlessly—called "nigger babies." Around Halloween time, the stores featured paraffin teeth and lips, along with bright orange paraffin harmonicas with pictures of witches and black cats pasted on the sides. Of course, all this seasonal paraphernalia was banned from school grounds and classrooms and teachers dutifully confiscated it.

By the end of the first three grades, most kids had managed to read, write, and do basic arithmetic. However, the most lasting impression was the worldview that the teachers laid out for us. Although ours was a public elementary school, there were daily reminders of God. We began each morning by reciting the Lord's Prayer, followed by the Pledge of Allegiance, which after 1953 included the words "under God." Some teachers added a Bible reading from the Protestant King James Version of 1611. The fact that the parents of Catholic students, who did not recognize the King James Bible, or that the parents of Jewish students, who did not regard Jesus as the Messiah, might object to these readings never seemed to enter the teachers' minds. One teacher went even further by asking all of us who went to Sunday school to raise our hands. She probably meant no harm, but her words again isolated the Catholic and Jewish kids, along with students who had little or no religious background (which the rest of us regarded with silent horror).

By leading us—back-to-back—in the Lord's Prayer and the Pledge of Allegiance, teachers made a firm connection between God and country. To them, the Constitutional separation between church and state was merely political and financial: The government could not create an official religion and the state could not spend tax dollars to support churches or religious schools. They took this to mean that public school teachers were free to say or do anything they wanted about religion in the classroom. Thus, on the far more potent level of ideas and concepts, they encouraged us to believe (as in church) that God and America were inseparable. Around Thanksgiving, teachers insisted that persecuted Protestants, who had fled the old country so they could worship freely in the New World, were the founders of our nation. Teachers had learned the same lessons a generation or two before and probably did not know that the historical record is far more complex. Nevertheless, their next step was to insist that America's continuing success depended on faith in God, reinforced by the Old Testament injunction, "Blessed is the nation whose God is the Lord." We were like the Jews of old, sent to a promised land to enjoy God's special blessings and to be His witnesses to all nations.

Chief among these blessings, according to teachers, was individual freedom. They said that America was the only place in the world where people could enjoy personal liberty or democratic government. This point of view left us to assume that other great democracies such as Canada, France, Australia, India, Israel, Great Britain, and many more were groaning under cruel dictators, kings, or other, lesser systems of government. Teachers similarly proposed that we were the best-educated people on earth, and that Americans had invented every modern device from television to rocket ships. That Henry Ford did not create the automobile, that Thomas Alva Edison did not discover electricity, or that Thomas Jefferson was not the first person to conceive of democracy would have come as a rude shock to us. The younger ones among us, after seeing Queen Elizabeth II on television, as she went through the streets of London in a horse-drawn carriage on her coronation day, concluded that the "backward" English still did not have motor cars.

What lay behind our teachers' distorted view of American history is not entirely clear. Perhaps it was mere postwar bombast, or part of a campaign to combat Communism during the Cold War. Maybe it was nothing more than a continuing attempt to support national identity in a country of immigrants who came from many lands. In any event, what teachers said about American history could sometimes verge on indoctrination. According to our textbooks, most immigrants had come to our country for political and religious liberty, despite overwhelming historical evidence that most had come, from the early 1600s to the present, for a better standard of living. The same textbooks unabashedly claimed that the United States had never started a war and had always pursued the noblest ideals in its foreign policy. The calculated slaughter of Native Americans was at best as the aberration of a few misguided military leaders rather than as a systematic national policy. Questions of racial hatred, ethnic discord, and high murder rates in the United States never surfaced at all.

Even if our teachers knew better, they would have hesitated to speak out at the height of the McCarthy era. In fact, our schools, and particularly our high school, took the Communist menace very seriously, and expended much time and energy exposing its very real defects. In retrospect, this anti-Communist crusade is understandable, especially if seen against the backdrop of World War II, when our nation had just spent so much blood and treasure to defeat Fascism. It seemed that we had no sooner brought down the Germans and Japanese than Communism reared its ugly head around the globe. We Americans, who have often held a simplistic view of evil, felt frustrated when one wicked gang had been defeated only to be replaced by another. The introduction of ever more destructive weapons in the form of atomic and hydrogen bombs now made the global scene more frustrating and frightening than ever, since even the most heroic acts might obliterate both sides.

We have many memories of the fear and distortion that infected our schools during those Cold War years. One is of regular air raid drills. At the sound of a bell (usually reserved for fire drills) we had to jump under our desks or run out into the hall and stand against the wall— depending on the civil defense strategy of the moment—to protect ourselves against a nuclear attack. As we stood there against the wall with our arms over our faces and heads or

cowering under desks, wondering how such puny precautions could ever protect us from hydrogen bombs, the principal paced up and down the long hall lecturing us on the evils of Communism.

During high school, the athletic awards assemblies offered the best opportunities for anti-Communist pep talks. Visiting speakers declared that football was an ideal training ground for combating the Red menace. They recalled how high-school football had prepared them for the rigors of World War II and, by implication, how it would condition us for the next great conflagration. Several times the principal followed up these remarks by quoting the probably apocryphal line from Duke of Wellington about how the Battle of Waterloo was won on the playing fields of Eton, his point being that the last great battle against the Communists had already begun on the playing fields of our high school.

Given this atmosphere, it is easy to understand why educators reacted with anger, disbelief, and determination when they heard that the Soviets had launched Sputnik, the first artificial satellite, in October 1957. As victims of their own misinformation, teachers, school administrators, and most other citizens assumed that the United States had always led the world in science and invention. Now it appeared that the Soviets had caught up with us and, far worse, had leapt ahead. The Communists' apparent lead in space also meant they had rockets powerful enough to rain nuclear warheads down on the United States from the Soviet Union itself. At the same time, their feats in space might convince the developing or nonaligned nations that Communism was superior to the American way of life. If the Soviets could launch Sputnik, there was simply no telling what other sinister plots they might have up their sleeves.

Across the country educators reacted to Sputnik with an orgy of self-castigation. There was only one reason for the Soviet lead in space, they concluded: hard though it was to believe, the Soviet educational system must be superior to our own. We therefore felt the pressure to study harder, especially when we received a new and more advanced high school physics textbook rushed into publication by some Ivy League professors in reaction to the Soviet challenge. The problem was that even the best students couldn't understand it, and we ended up learning less about physics than students learned the year before, with their supposedly inferior texts.

Another result of this hysterical reaction to Sputnik was an intensification of fears about the world at large. The school therefore stepped up its opposition to dissent and the free exchange of ideas. Indeed, the whole atmosphere at school ran counter to the nation's commitment to individual liberty. Contradictorily, many teachers applauded what they liked to call "rugged individualism," but what they really had in mind was economic competition rather than conflicting opinions. In the same way, English teachers praised Henry David Thoreau for his independent spirit, but they would have been horrified if any of us had taken up Thoreau's ideas on civil disobedience. What teachers and administrators wanted was unquestioning conformity to small town, middle-class values—as they understood them.

This insistence on conformity extended to the high-school newspaper. It carried such items as "The Student of the Week," predictably about an unimaginative kid who made good grades and was active in a host of official school clubs. There was a story on sports, a laudatory review of the most recent assembly speaker, and maybe an opinion piece on proper school dress or the need for better costumes in school plays. The newspaper's faculty advisor would not allow articles that even remotely questioned community standards or school rules.

In these ways, the student body was expected to mirror the values and attitudes held by adults in town, and this included social class rankings. Not surprisingly, the leading student clique comprised the sons and daughters of doctors, lawyers, and corporate managers. From this same circle came most of the student council representatives, club officers, prom queens, and cheerleaders. Even more damaging, some of the high-school counselors assumed that the sons and daughters of factory workers had no interest in going to college and advised them to follow a vocational program in high school.

Fortunately, not all our teachers went along with the program. One was a young civics teacher who came to the high school in the early 1960s. He had reddish-blond hair and a boyish face that seemed to echo his enthusiasm for the subject. Unlike the others who taught civics, he gave liberals and conservatives equal time in his lectures and classroom discussions, and even invited a Democratic congressman (in a town that was overwhelmingly Republican) to speak to the class. Best of all, he organized lively debates among students on controversial issues such as civil rights, social welfare, foreign aid, and free speech. We later heard that he decided to quit high-school teaching and to earn a Ph.D. in political science so he could teach in college. We would not have been surprised to learn that he had been asked to leave the high school.

Under the circumstances, most teachers stayed away from current events and concentrated on teaching their subjects. One of these was a biology teacher who approached the subject with such humor that sitting in his class could make us forget we were in school. A geometry teacher helped us to remember certain concepts with jokes, some of which were not funny at all, but which somehow stuck. One of the more memorable ones went like this: "What did one little triangle say to the other little triangle when it started to rain?" Answer: "Let's coincide." Looking back, the joke seems to have had sexual connotations, something that may or may not have struck our prim female instructor.

Of course, high school was much more than classrooms and patriotic assemblies. One of the high points was ·the annual October bonfire and pep rally. The band marched in full regalia from the high school to the county fairgrounds, passing through the downtown on the way, blasting our fight song along the whole route. By the time the band and the crowd of followers reached the site, the bonfire was already lit and roaring in the cool autumn night, illuminating the entire western section of the fairgrounds and lighting the faces of hundreds of students with a reddish-orange glow. Facing the blaze was a flatbed farm wagon that served as a platform for the coaches and players. The coaches jumped up first to proclaim that everyone was in fighting spirit for the big game. Then they introduced several of the star players who vowed maiming and death to the enemy. The cheerleaders let loose with a rousing yell, to be following by another blast from the band. The climax came when a "player" from the opposition team was thrown into the fire and burned in effigy.

The big game took place the next night, which was always Friday. Football being tremendously popular in our part of the country, several thousand people jammed themselves into our small athletic field. Besides the spectators in the stands, there were dozens of fans sitting and standing in old garages or barn lofts that bordered the field along a narrow alley on one side. Behind the end zone fence there was always a row or two of local men, the same

210

old timers who had come there for years, second guessing the coaches and remembering the older brothers—or even the fathers—of current pig skin heroes.

To run out onto that field, wearing the colors of our high school, and hearing the roar of the crowd was enough to sustain many players for decades. The football boys had been prepared, almost brutally, for the entire week by a coaching staff who wouldn't let them drink any water during practice, and who did everything they could to provoke their most violent instincts. In fact, this training began well before the football season when they reported in early August for "conditioning" in the high-school gym. There, every night, team members played a game called murder ball. The coach tossed a football, basketball, or simple playground ball into the middle of 65 boys, each wanting to prove his worth as a player. Everyone tried to grab the ball and then to slaughter any kid who got hold of it, wresting him to the floor and forcing it out of his hands, at which point the victor became the next victim of mass attack. On into each August night, they played this brutal game, as more and more players staggered home with bloody noses, gashed arms and legs, multiple floor burns, and huge bruises. After several weeks of this punishment, the coaches thought the team was ready to go out into the hot afternoon sun for two-a-day practices in full gear. Many players vomited, and it is a miracle no one died of heat exhaustion. Yet in the atmosphere of those days, these hard-driving coaches became heroes, father figures who were much more demanding than dads ever dared to be at home.

Of course, football was the only sport that really mattered in town, with basketball a distant second. Maybe because football demanded a warlike determination, many townspeople lavished the sort of attention on football stars they usually reserved for war heroes. Anyway, it could be pleasantly unsettling for a star player to walk downtown on a Saturday morning after a successful game the night before and to be greeted in awe by the local shoe store owner or a girlfriend's father. It was an exhilarating image that many players revisited in private moments for years to come.

Besides football and basketball—and far down on the list of popularity—our high school offered only three other interscholastic sports. They were baseball, track, and golf—for boys alone. Girls had to accept an auxiliary role as cheerleaders, band members, homecoming queens, or fans in the stands. Maybe our community saw this arrangement as preparation to become helpmates to husbands later in life. Yet our mothers remembered there had been a girls' interscholastic basketball team in the 1920s and 1930s that did very well in competition. It was a sign of our own cramped era, when women enjoyed fewer opportunities than a generation before, that none of us thought to ask what had become of the girls' basketball team or to suggest that it might be resurrected. Some girls may have secretly raged that they had no athletic opportunities, but if any had voiced such anger, we would have thought them as odd as three-dollar bills.

Often after these male-only athletic contests, there was a sock hop in the gym. There were also special dances like the one on Homecoming Weekend or the Junior and Senior Proms. The girls spent a whole week before these events decorating the gym with crepe paper and covering the fold out bleachers (now folded in) with pastel drawings of woodland scenes. The theme became more elaborate in a small area around the prom queen's throne, put together with the help of artificial trees and shrubs borrowed from the window display supplies of a local department store and artificial grass from one of the funeral homes, which used this fake turf to disguise the bare earth beside graves during burial services.

Girls arrived at theses dances in heavily crinolined gowns that stuck almost straight out from their waists, each with a small corsage purchased by their dates. We boys wore our best Sunday suits and carefully polished shoes. None of us would have considered renting a tuxedo, let alone arriving in a limousine. Nor were there any plans for topping off the evening with a lavish dinner and maybe an early morning visit to a sleazy motel, all standard practice in urban areas just a decade or two later. In addition, no one ever imagined holding the dance in a hotel ballroom or country club, a common expectation in our own kids' generation. Even if our parents could have afforded such excesses, they, as well as school authorities, would have nixed them in the name of good behavior and good taste. A midnight or one o'clock curfew, immediately after the dance was over, also ruled out sexual adventures on prom night.

These fun activities associated with school, like much that we experienced at home, stood in sharp contrast to a dangerous and contradictory world. Rather, they were part of a safe and self-affirming life that fortunately coexisted with the terrors of Cold War America. But by distorting the realities of our time, and especially by failing to question the racial, religious, and gender stereotypes of our day, many of our educators gave us little notion of the world that beckoned on the other side of graduation.

7. Rites of Passage

We're amazed at how much freedom our parents gave us to spend all day roaming the woods and hills that rimmed the town. Some of our haunts took us several miles away, to places where there was no way to call home in those days, before anyone even thought of smart phones. Loaded down with army surplus canteens and backpacks filled with pretzels, peanut butter sandwiches, and cookies, we often headed out in the morning for an area known as Flatrocks, so-called because of its sandstone cliffs and steep drop-offs. Heavily wooded and overlooking the local cemetery, Flatrocks was once the site of a quarry, where a few years after the Civil War stone

for the county courthouse had been blasted and chiseled out of the cliffs. Another favorite haunt was a sheer, sandstone bluff that rose 250 feet or so above the county fairgrounds. Its higher climbs were more exciting, but it was our second choice because of the tourists and sightseers who always got in the way.

After reaching one of these hideouts, we broke into groups for war games. Our "enemies" were Nazis or Japanese, the Communists not being as recognizable as the German and Japanese soldiers we had seen in dozens of war movies. Another game was Indians and frontiersmen. Most of us wanted to be Indians (at a time when "Native American had not entered our vocabulary), since they could terrify with their screams or move with incredible stealth. Besides, the remains of their culture were all around us. Up and down the cliffs were a series of hand and footholds that members of a local tribe had chiseled into the rocks long before we came along. We imagined braves crawling along the ledges and scrambling up and down from one level to another. We sometimes even stumbled on arrowheads. Local lore held that Indians had used a cave hollowed out by wind and rain thousands of years before as a shelter and lookout. We imagined ourselves running along the same trails and leaping over narrow chasms in pursuit of white intruders. In a community where white supremacy was taken for granted to one degree or another, this attitude seems strange now, and might be explained by the fact that there were no longer any Native Americans in our midst. At the same time, we could admire them for their bravery and woodland skills in contrast to our own more prosaic lives.

In fact, so many of us wanted to be Indian braves that we often divided into rival tribes. It was irrelevant that none of them had lived in our part of the country. What mattered was the trill of sneaking up on the enemy, overpowering him with a ferocious yell and shooting him dead. The only thing better was pretending to die an agonizing and dramatic death. Only later would we recognize that impersonating Native Americans was racist and understandably objectionable.

As we got older these battles against various imaginary "enemies" grew more realistic, with rock fights and wrestling matches. Once we mustered enough courage to have a BB gun fight. Firing "real" ammunition only added to the thrill. Remembering our mothers' warnings about shooting someone's eyes out with BB guns, we agreed to fire only below the belt. The deal lasted only until somebody was "bloodied," and we went all the way, shooting at whatever moved.

Serious battles required building huts and fortifications out of dead timber and live brush. These projects took several days to complete, with trips home for supper and bed. Our parents' great trust, coupled with living in an exceedingly safe community, allowed such juvenile teamwork, but it was not an experience we wanted for our own children a generation later.

Other favorite playgrounds were the miles of alleys that ran between streets all over town. Paved with gravel, or sometimes just covered with dirt or grass, the alleys were originally for access to the barns and stables behind almost every house during the horse and buggy days. Many of these outbuildings were still there, most crudely converted into garages. The alleys attracted us because they were public property and therefore seemed to belong to no one. In our minds, an alley could become a road through the wilderness, a mean city street, or a hidden landing strip inside Nazi Germany. Later, alleys were great places to walk with a date at night. With or without a girlfriend, a walk through the alleys after dark was a means of seeing what was going on in the back parts of your neighbors' houses without revealing yourself.

Scouting was a more organized version of childhood play. While the younger Cub Scouts stayed close to home, Boy Scout troops took to the woods and hills whenever they had the chance. Scoutmasters taught us camping skills, which included pitching tents, building campfires, digging latrines, cooking over open fires, and protecting ourselves from rain and the other elements. They also passed on a body of woodland lore that extended to tracking animals in the snow or finding our way out of a thicket. In the end, we always wondered how we'd ever use this information. Although we have long forgotten most of these lessons, scouting professed to offer what psychologists like to call male bonding rituals.

Whatever the case, much of this ritual involved a lot of juvenile silliness, and sometimes thoughtless cruelty. Once we filled Donny Cadbury's sleeping bag with Cheez Whiz. On another camping trip, a kid "peed" into another scout's simmering chicken noodle soup. These were random stupidities, but one kid in our scout troop named Benny Kizer became the butt of cruel pranks. Benny was a little overweight with always messed-up hair. Today there would be a name for Benny's condition, maybe some sort of emotional disability. Benny got into our troop because some well-meaning soul probably thought scouting might help him to adjust. Back then, when no one talked of "mainstreaming," we failed to appreciate his handicap and simply thought he was dumb, in the sense of being innocent or naive. He believed anything we told him. "Hey Benny," we'd say, "Did you hear the governor is coming to pass out free firecrackers downtown?" Or, "Did you know we're all getting free tickets to a professional baseball game?" And he believed us.

Benny was also an unorthodox Boy Scout. On camping trips, he brought along strange gear, strange, that is, to all of us who had bought the entire regulation assemblage of axes, compasses, mess kits, bedding, and a dozen other pieces of official paraphernalia. Instead of a sleeping bag, Benny lugged in three or four blankets. In place of the efficient, military-style cooking equipment, he brought a skillet from his mom's pantry; and instead of the traditional eggs and bacon, he came laden with cans of mushroom soup.

At our age, we couldn't appreciate Benny's uniqueness, and we resorted to the cruelties of many eleven and twelve-year-old boys toward anyone who was different. It didn't matter that Benny slept as well under his four blankets as we did in our more expensive, Boy-Scout-approved sleeping bags; and his mushroom soup and crackers were at least as efficient and filling as our eggs, bacon, and burnt bread. Perhaps what upset us most was his challenge to the security we had from doing everything by the book, like everyone else in the troop.

It was inevitable that our teasing of Benny would escalate. One night some of the older boys pulled him out of his blankets, stripped him down to his underwear, and hung him upside down over the side of a cliff. His screams woke the rest of us, who managed to free him. Our scout leaders, worn out by the constant mayhem surrounding Benny, decided not to punish the perpetrators, but to dismiss the victim instead. None of us knew what looks passed over Benny's face when he heard the news. What heartaches he must have suffered, we can only guess, for he was no longer with us. A couple of Monday nights after that, as we were going into the church basement for our weekly Scout meeting, we saw Benny riding past on his bicycle. He repeated this sad journey every Monday for what seemed like months, innocently waving at the boys who were not too ashamed to look up at him.

For the rest of us, there were more camping trips to enjoy. The high point came at night around a big campfire. With the flames flickering in our faces and throwing shadows against the dark woods, and with animals rustling in the distance or calling out among the trees, we listened to gruesome ghost stories and tall tales. One assistant scoutmaster liked to tell stories about his experiences as a pilot in the Pacific theater during World War II. We heard about headhunters in New Guinea, ritual sacrifices by the natives, and giant snakes falling from trees.

Such stories seemed natural in a scouting program that was quasi-militaristic in looks as well as in spirit. The smart uniforms and salutes made us feel very soldierly in this after wash of World War II. Scouting's emphasis on order and rank also appealed to us, as did the scout knives, bows and arrows, and survival training—military type factors that the national organization well understood. We were therefore shocked to hear that Bobby Root's mother forbade him to join the Boy Scouts because of its obvious militaristic side. Bobby was her only child, and she "was not going to have any son of mine join an organization that is part of a sneaky plan to get boys ready for war." As proof, she pointed to the survival training, the uniforms, the salutes, and all the badges of rank. She probably reflected the fears of many mothers in those days, when war followed upon war and the promise of new conflicts loomed just over the horizon. But to us, she was both silly and unfair.

What no one brought up, however, was the stark reality that there were no African American members of our scout troop, or any other troops in town. Nor did we have any Black playmates—or playmates from any minority group. This situation was partly because the population of our town was overwhelmingly white. Even though one could argue that the segregation was largely by default, we were still deprived of having any life-affirming relationships with those who were outwardly different from us.

While the Scouts organized boyish adventures very well, it was probably unnecessary for us, who already had plenty of time and outdoor space to organize ourselves. We created secret clubs at about the same age we entered the Boy Scouts, meeting in some kid's basement or back barn. Once a group of neighborhood kids set up a clubhouse in a shed, a small, abandoned workshop attached to the rear of a wood frame house that belonged to one of the member's grandmothers. On the door, we painted a skull-and-crossbones, with the solemn warning scrawled underneath, "Death to Trespassers." With a membership of eight to ten boys, we held weekly "business meetings" all summer. The main agenda was constantly electing a new "captain," the title we gave to our leader, since no one was ever satisfied with the boy we had elected the week before. Then we drank a pitcher of Kool Aid, which pretty much ended the business meeting.

Our chief reason for existing as a club was to fight off the attacks of rival clubs. Combat began with loud insults and pounding against the clubhouse door, followed by a shower of rocks and sticks against the outside walls. Slipping out though a trapdoor in the floor, we met the enemy and waged battle. The weapon of choice for both sides was a two-foot-long willow twig about the thickness of our little fingers. We kept a pile of these in the clubhouse, sharpened on one end and ready for combat. Onto these points, we stuck small green apples, which were lying all over the yard. If aimed properly and whipped with enough force, the apples inflicted a bad sting and left a bruise that lasted for several days. The key was accuracy, a skill that neither side mastered despite all the battles. Most of us were interested in whipping the apple off the stick as fast as possible, and a hit was an unexpected thrill. Sometimes we were outmaneuvered and discovered that our enemies had invaded the clubhouse and were tearing it apart. After one of these disasters, we were sure to elect a new captain the following week.

Our animosity toward this other group, who lived just a few blocks away, was really contrived for the sake of adventure. After the fight both sides got together to finish off the Kool-Aid. Sometimes one of our members sneaked into his blind grandfather's house and stole cigars right under the old man's nose. The clubhouse soon filled with a foul blue smoke as we puffed away on our own White Owls and pretended to be men relaxing after a great battle. More than once a kid got sick on a cigar and puked all over the yard.

Other exploits reflected the early days of the country's space age. Our friend George's family had a firing range in a dugout extension of the basement. The range was for his father and older brother to use, while George himself was banned because he was "too young."

Even so, their target shooting in the middle of town in an under-house bunker did not seem at all strange at the time when some people were starting to build nuclear fallout shelters. His family's interest in guns also provided us a store of gunpowder, which we occasionally filched in small amounts. At first, George just put the powder out on the lawn and touched a match to it. Soon we came up with bigger and better ideas, such as building our own miniature rockets.

We filled a paper drinking straw with gunpowder, leaving just enough room at one end to twist it into a tail, and plugged the other end with a small piece of willow twig. We then loaded this slim missile into one end of a long metal pipe and lit the tail with a match, watching excitedly as it whistled across lawns, swooping and diving, until the sudden burnout. Puffed up with success, we found a second pipe and split into teams, firing these unguided missiles at each other across lawns and back alleys. One of the neighbors called the police, who took to cruising the alleys and streets in our neighborhood more than usual. The end of our missile careers came when George's father noticed the missing gunpowder, resulting in a whipping for George and a padlock on the firing range door.

The seedbed for many of these ideas was the movies. Our town supported four downtown theaters, and one outdoor drive-in known as the Skyview Cruise In. "Movie" was the operative word, since we thought only snobs and film critics talked about "cinema," "film," or "motion pictures." Our standard fare in those days was on the same level as the television sitcoms and the evening soap operas of the era—that were turned out just as fast. Yet there was something magical about sitting in a darkened theater with kids from all over town.

Our favorite movie time was Saturday afternoon, when admission for those under 14 was only ten cents.

Before the double feature began, there were six or seven cartoons, one right after another. We saw Popeye, Tom and Jerry, Bugs Bunny, Daffy Duck, and other animated characters in one violent scene after the next, which we thought quite normal and that our parents accepted without examination. Then came a western thriller with Roy Rogers, Gene Autry, or Hopalong Cassidy—movies a decade old even then. The second feature, for the same ten cents, was usually a grade "B" number about World War II.

By then Hollywood was feeling the competition from television and fought back with several gimmicks. These included great Bible epics, quasi-religious blockbusters like *Ben-Hur* and *The Robe*; 3-D, which required us to wear polarized glasses made of plastic and cardboard; wider screens, known as Cinemascope; and a type of bingo called Screeno, which drew crowds who hoped to leave the theater entertained as well as a few dollars richer.

None of these gimmicks held our attention as much as sitting in afternoon darkness watching an old Roy Rogers movie as he sang and slugged his way through a gang of mustachioed bad guys. Still, we wondered at the contradiction between his fighting it out in old-time saloons and riding horses, while having easy access to Jeeps, airplanes, and telephones. If it were not Roy, it was John Wayne beating the Japanese on Iwo Jima; Lyle Bettger hunting down wicked agents who sold guns and whiskey to the Indians; or Jeff Chandler testing the latest Jet fighters for the Korean War. Science fiction thrillers were also regular Saturday fare, like *The Day the World Stood Still, Invasion of the Body Snatchers*, *The Thing*, and *War of the Worlds*. We knew from the beginning that even the U.S. Army was useless against the hideous creatures that stalked the screen. Once the beast appeared, the whole point of watching was to find out what or who would finally do it in. The favored weapons against such monsters were microscopic bacteria, true love, or even God.

As we walked home in the gathering darkness of a winter afternoon, we picked up sticks and pretended to be one of the characters in the movie just seen. We swaggered along, quoting the most bombastic lines of the movie ("Watch out for those teeth, Commander, they're like giant swords!") and ray-gunning each other while wandering over backyards and brick sidewalks lined with huge sycamore trees.

While sex was taboo in the movies then, violence was always part of the drama. It was not the violence itself that was harmful, but the misleading way it was depicted: War movies showed men who were shot in such a way that only a small hole appeared on the body, accompanied by just a few drops of blood. Only later did we realize that war resulted in men being blown apart or decapitated, in having their intestines spewed all over the ground, or in having huge holes shot through their stomachs, arms, and legs. Fist fights in western movies that lasted for three or four minutes produced only a cut lip and slightly messed up hair. Again, it was only later when we discovered that fistfights, with full-swinging blows to the chin, could shatter a person's jaw and result in a coma or death. In this sense, the violence we saw on Saturday afternoons at the movies was both misleading and dangerous.

Most of the movie stars of that era are long forgotten. However, when we were growing up, they were All-American heroes, who, like the nation at large, acted out a self-appointed mission to uphold righteousness and conquer evil. Although this was a distorted view of humanity, which fed the worst delusions of our super patriots, these Saturday afternoon potboilers let us imagine that one courageous man acting alone could overcome all the dark forces of our postwar world.

Students of American culture have made much of the 1956 science fiction movie, *Invasion of the Body Snatchers*. Set in a small town not unlike our own, it was the story of strange pods that appeared at victims' houses and gradually, as the person slept, "took over" the inner self. Outwardly, the victims were the same, but their souls had been snatched away, sparing only a zombielike county agent, school secretary, or clergyman. The hero of the film, a local doctor played by Kevin McCarthy, begins a search for this insidious force, which so quietly and unobtrusively has robbed him of neighbors and friends. The movie's connection with fears of creeping Communism, and what we had been taught about its equally insidious "brain washing," was hard to miss.

We gained more realistic insights about life when we landed our first jobs. We cousins took turns as newspaper boys. We delivered the local paper Monday through Saturday to about 150 houses, collected payment every Saturday morning, and earned three or four dollars a week (worth 30 to 40 dollars six decades later). One of our dads was the editor of the newspaper, causing us to feel we were helping him in some small way.

Perhaps the most valuable lesson from being a paperboy was personal discipline. Whatever else we were doing, we had to stop at 3:30 in the afternoon to deliver the evening paper, a real sacrifice when it meant giving up after school activities or leaving the swimming pool on a hot summer day while friends could stay for a couple more hours. We also learned a lot about our neighbors: Some customers were scrupulous about settling their 35-cent accounts once a week, while others did everything possible to avoid our collection-day visits. Even casual observations revealed if someone had drunk too much the night before on the front porch swing because of the beer cans littering the floor. Sometimes couples argued so loudly we could hear them through the front door; or their discussions told of a husband who had lost his job that week.

One of us graduated from the paper route to a job after school in the newspaper's mailing room. The mailing room employees received the print runs from the pressroom a floor below, then counted and tied them up for the carriers, or addressed single copies for postal subscribers. Many of the pressmen, along with the mailing room boss, were tough working guys who filled the air with the foulest language we had ever heard. The boss not only swore like a sailor, but also amused himself by putting obscene signs on the mailing room door when he went out to lunch, hoping one of the young female secretaries in the circulation department would come by and couldn't avoid seeing it. The worst of these was the cartoon of a man with his mouth wide open and about to bite into a woman's large, naked breast. Below the picture in bold letters were the words, "OUT TO LUNCH!"—behavior that in a later era would have at the very least resulted in his well-deserved firing. In addition, the boss also swore wildly whenever the circulation manager came back with some new order, and verbally abused the poor fellow even more behind his back, giving us some firsthand knowledge of the cruder side of labor-management relations.

Another job, especially desired by high school athletes, was summer construction. One of us landed such a coveted job with a local contractor. The owner agreed to the hire only if we understood that the wage was 50 cents an hour, paid in cash with no reporting to the federal government. It was a non-union firm, and thus the regular workers were not especially skilled at digging foundations, carrying hod, or unloading delivery trucks full of bricks or sacks of concrete. The men, married young and saddled with two or three mouths to feed, talked about nothing but women (called "koosh"), getting drunk, and somehow escaping to Florida to work "year-round." Our project chief, the owner's brother, was a mason by trade and chewed tobacco incessantly. His trademark was to spit a heavily laced tobacco glob in the corner of a sidewalk as he laid down the final touches with his trowel. The brown spot remained for months. The only real lesson from such a summer job was that, unless you were a skilled tradesman, there could be no greater incentive for going to college.

If we learned from customers, bosses, and fellow employees something about the life of labor, we had only each other to find out about the most burning subject of all—sex. Our parents, who told us little or nothing about the subject, probably trusted that somehow, through the normal progression of things, we would find out on our own. The result was that our ignorance about sex was monumental. Depending on which schoolyard philosopher we listened to, we believed that masturbation could make hair (or warts) grow on the palms of our hands and eventually lead to blindness, impotence, or both. Our Catholic friends were told that masturbation was a mortal sin that could be expiated only through the confessional booth. We also heard that acne was a sign of syphilis, that girls who crossed their legs and bounced their foot were "asking for it", and that wearing "brief" underwear could make you sterile or even "queer."

One consequence of this ignorance was an atmosphere of darkness surrounding the whole subject of sex. We overheard stories from parents and other adults about a local man who "liked boys," or about two women who shared a house, or about the unexplained six-month visit of a neighborhood girl to her aunt in Nebraska, or about a girl who suddenly dropped out of school part way through the year. There were also whispers about a married embalmer who paid regular evening calls on a "widow lady" down the block. This tale prompted some women in town to speak bitingly of not wanting to be sent over to his funeral parlor after they were dead, where the philandering undertaker might "find out what I have under my skirts." These stories never made much sense to us—only that something shady was probably going on. It took us years to figure out whom they were talking about and what they meant.

Having gown-up in this secretive and forbidden atmosphere, our parents must have felt their innards seize up every time they had to address the subject of sex in front of us. However, unlike their parents, who refused to say anything at all to them on the subject, our moms and dads in that era thought they had to give some sort of instruction. When Dad thought the right moment had come, he said, "Let's have a talk after dinner, upstairs in your room." Sensing that something ominous and uncomfortable was coming, we mumbled our assent. Once upstairs amidst the clutter of model airplanes, high school pennants, and old comic books, Dad went through a form of speech failure and began stuttering out his dreaded lines: "Uh, ahh, umm, tell me son, have you learned anything—I mean are you aware of—do they teach you anything at school, . . . anything at all about, ah, the facts, as it were, of, uh, life, so to speak; the basics of, ahmmm, the reproductive system?" Thinking about the little bit of biology and general science we had learned (none of which had much to say about human reproduction) we sheepishly answered, "Well sort of."

"Ah good, then that settles that," said Dad with great relief. Back downstairs, he went with a light heart and an even lighter conscience, where he reassured Mom that he had performed the dreadful duty to the satisfaction of us both.

Other parents we knew attacked the problem of sex education by handing their teenage kids a book about the facts of life, written by some doctor or psychologist in stilted clinical language. We thought that even these manuals were wicked, since their parents warned them to keep the books to themselves and not to share them with friends whose parents might not approve. When one of our friends received such a book, the first thing he did was to pass it around the neighborhood. One night we sat on his front porch reading it with a flashlight. Terrified that some adult would appear, we were careful to wrap the forbidden volume in the dust jacket of an old western novel by Zane Gray. The book did help to dispel some of our more ridiculous ideas about sex, but we remained in the dark about exactly how people performed the sex act, to say nothing of the emotional dimensions of a sexual encounter.

Catholic high school students did receive some instruction about relations between the sexes that was out of sync with the times, and that would have been so, even in our parents' generation. A double-sided printed message from their priest began with the bold heading, "NO-NECK CLUB." The first rule of the club read, "At the outset of every date we will exchange the password—"NO-NECK." Further down, club members were directed to ask themselves, "What would Christ do on a date? How would Mary the Virgin react on a date?" Historically and culturally, the questions were ludicrous, given that dating did not exist in first century Palestine. Anyway, the reaction to the "NO-NECK CLUB" from the boys we knew was one of scoffing and derision and it therefore did nothing to help reveal the realities of sex.

Meanwhile, no one even broached the subject of same-sex relationships. This was a forbidden subject that we discovered only gradually, and then, unfortunately, through the crudest kind of name calling and jokes. Of the hundreds of classmates, friends, or acquaintances, there had to have been some who were gay, bisexual, or transgender. Years later, we learned that a classmate and friend was gay only after he died of AIDS in a distant city. He must have endured a very painful life in the shadows, unable to be himself.

Eventually, we did get down the basic facts about sex between a man and a woman. We knew the two had to get together to have a baby, but we were still unsure about how that happened and how the baby came out. Some of the boys thought that intercourse meant that the man peed in the woman's rectum and that the baby came out from there. We guys just jawed around about it and finally, with the help of some older brothers, we put together how it all worked. We also speculated endlessly during high school about which girls would have sex, or "put out," as we phrased it. This wild guessing went on for hours as we fed our fantasies. We would shoot baskets behind some kid's garage while mulling over the latest gossip, often letting our imaginations run wild and making up tales as we went along. This was the worst sort of objectification, but without any guidance in the larger emotional context of sexual activity, we only managed to discuss the physical side.

The braver guys went as far as to buy condoms—"rubbers" as we called them—to carry around and show off in this era before the "pill." They could be bought out of a vending machine in certain gas stations around town, usually in one of the greasier places located on major highways that catered to truck drivers. The condoms were uniformly a milky white color, the fancier ones with a reservoir tip. Various sizes appeared in print on the top of the package, but we doubted even then if the Trojan Company made anything smaller than the large size, or that any boy would admit to needing a more diminutive size, even if they were available. Few of us ever used these latex trophies but flashing a condom as we opened our billfolds was an important rite of passage.

In fact, the best birth control came from hearing that a classmate "had gotten herself pregnant" (or, more crudely, "had gotten knocked up") and then witnessing the shock waves as word spread through the high school and community at large. The girls had to leave school immediately; walking out of the building (as we imagined her) with head hung low in darkening shame. The young father, whether the couple married or not, could finish his education but fared little better as he became a pariah to most of his old friends. In our minds, both of the "guilty" parties had passed from youthful innocence into some hard, obligatory land where no one ever snake-danced at a bonfire again. The boy usually gave up all extracurricular activities to work after school and into the evening. One boy we knew was a potential All-State football player with a college scholarship in the offing when his girlfriend made the terrible announcement that she was pregnant. No one questioned that he would have to quit the team and give up any thoughts of college football to go to work to support the mother and baby. Given the double standard of the time, the girl suffered much more moral opprobrium than her boyfriend did.

Besides being scared to death about pregnancy, most of us, boys and girls alike, thought premarital sex was morally wrong. Our parents' fears were partly at the bottom of this. Necking, petting, or "making out," as we called these activities, were acceptable, but even here girls did not want the reputation of being "too fast" or "hot." Boys often exaggerated their exploits as lovers, and frequent tales of wanton sex filtered back to the girls themselves, with the result that the boy found it hard to get a date with anyone "respectable." One of our high school English teachers, who was unmarried and lived with her bachelor brother, went even further to link "illicit sex" with everlasting disgrace. Once a year she said to the girls in her classes, in a voice that sounded a bit like Eleanor's Roosevelt's, "Just remember, girls, a moment of pleasure is not worth a life in shame." Where and how she picked up such a high-pitched, aristocratic accent in our small town, or why this proper maiden lady thought it her duty to warn against sexual impropriety, remains a puzzle to this day.

Community mores also held that it was the girls' duty to "draw the line" and keep the boys from "going too far." This made sense, since she was the one who would get pregnant and become the greater object of shame. So powerful was this rule that it never reached the level of open debate, the girls objecting to it only during private "gripe sessions."

Despite the fear and double standards, some kids did have sex in high school and some girls we knew did become pregnant. Even our mothers were aware of at least three girls in their neighborhood who became pregnant out of wedlock back in the 1930s. Curiously, none of them married the fathers. One girl went off to an unwed mothers' home in the state capital and put her child up for adoption; the other two had their babies in town and allowed their parents to adopt them. In our own day, all the girls we knew married the boys with whom they had become pregnant, an indication of the widespread approval of early marriage during these prosperous postwar years. Despite the marriages, such pregnancies were still somewhat scandalous, but within another generation, having a child while unmarried would raise few eyebrows anywhere. For some, it was a positive choice.

Dating in our teen years amounted to a cheap night at the movies. "Dinner" meant going to one of the drive-in restaurants, our favorite being a place called Jimmy's. It was the home of Jimmy's Jawbreaker, a large double-decker hamburger loaded with onions, pickles, tomatoes, plenty of salt, and a sauce bursting with secret ingredients. The Friday night dances at the YMCA were also dating possibilities, but they were more for picking up a date than for taking one. Live music at the "Y" dances came from Rick Thimble and his four-piece band. Their heyday had been in the thirties and forties, and their specialties were the swing tunes of our parents' young adulthoods. They struggled to play rock and roll tunes on instruments from the big band era, but they more commonly tried to update an old favorite like "Glow Worm" or "Blue Moon." Even then, they failed on almost every note. Some of us sarcastically referred to the group as "Rick Thimble and his Syncopated Record Player."

Fortunately for the band, we paid little attention to the music. Nor did the ugliness of the "Y" premises, located in an old National Guard armory near downtown, keep us from having a good time. The armory was a hideous yellow-gray color on the outside and equally drab inside, later reminding us of pictures of a police station in Franco's Spain. The dances took place in a large gymnasium on the main floor, which smelled of sweat, shoe polish, old varnish, and gun oil.

The point of these evenings at the "Y" was the chance to see and be seen. Once kids moved onto the dance floor, we knew in a minute who had the right stuff. Some guys were smooth and moved easily from girl to girl— smiling, laughing, and being admired by both sexes. The luckier girls were asked to dance time after time and were even lined up in advance. However, most of us, boys as well as girls, stood in clumps on the sidelines of the gym floor, talking to friends of the same sex. Often, we spent the entire night in one spot, or suddenly moved away in a bunch, like some chowder-and-marching society, from a foothold by the wall to the Coke machine in the hall, or out onto the front steps of the armory and then back to our post on the sidelines. Occasional brief gasps filled the nearby air as one of the girls was asked to dance—or there were cheerful guffaws as one of our friends got up enough guts to approach some girl he had been talking about all evening.

However, the very best place to attract attention was the county fair. This event came in the middle of October and will always be associated in our minds with burning leaves and high-school football games. Our town's schools declared a three-day holiday for the fair, while students from the surrounding villages and farms received the whole week off. All week long, the fairgrounds were clogged with great packs of boys and girls, roaming and smiling, taking each other on rides, or talking to the 4-H kids who were tending their animals in various barns. In the process, many teenage romances sprouted between kids who had been total strangers at the beginning of the week.

A Sweet-Corn Festival, held in early September in a village north of town, was another weeklong event that brought boys and girls together. Students wandered the fairways in groups wearing their high-school letter sweaters and jackets as a sign of loyalty. This moving parade, with its bright mixture of odd-colored school regalia was not unlike a medieval university pageant in which members of the assorted colleges displayed their gowns while marching through town. In counterpoint to this exalted procession of youngsters on the prowl were the great vats of boiling sweet corn and other "eats" served up by the mothers of local booster clubs and service organizations.

When it came to the solitary date, access to a car was an absolute necessity. Understandably, more than one sociologist has credited the automobile with vast changes in courtship habits in the twentieth century. Cars allowed only cramped quarters for adolescent romances, but they were both private and mobile. With a car, we could drive out along some deserted country road where neither parents nor neighbors could see us or disapprove, there to explore the mysteries of sexual intimacy. We suspect that a high percentage of pre-pill marriages came from of such escapades in the country.

A car could also take us to the drive-in movie, a boom industry during the generation after World War II. Known as "passion pits," the drive-ins were popular places for young teenagers to do their groping and kissing in supposed privacy as others watched the movie—or did the same thing. Wherever we went, whether to drive-ins or out on dusty country roads, our dream was a Nash Rambler. We heard the Rambler's front seat went down all the way to make a sort of bed where lovers could carry on their clandestine acts in real comfort.

We also wanted a car so we could go cruising around town on weekends at the height of the postwar car culture. All sorts of vehicles loaded with teenagers floated up and down the streets on Friday and Saturday nights, with kids yelling at each other from open windows or arranging to swap riders. Boys from one car jumped in with a load of girls from another, while some of the girls went over the boys' car. The more crowded the cars, the better, since we then had to sit as close as possible, or better, still; the girls would have to sit on our laps. Our destinations on cruising nights were the drive-in restaurants. We drove slowly through the parking lots and looked for friends or someone we had a crush on from school. When things got slow in town, we gathered several carloads for a run up to the amusement park at the lake.

Cars could also become dangerous toys. Drag racing was a common pastime on a narrow straightaway out in the country—or even on city streets. Some drivers played "chicken," a game that required the driver of a packed car to tear along the highway at a high speed with his hands off the steering wheel. The chicken became the first person inside the car to grab the wheel as the car careened along the road.

Cars also gave teenagers an identity, especially to the few who had enough money to buy their own "wheels."

They often modified ("chopped and channeled" in the lingo of the day) their prized vehicles to create a low-slung chariot with rumbling glass-packed mufflers. They belonged to the kinds of boys who knew how to tinker with cars and keep them in tip-top repair. The rest of us were stuck with the family car, a necessary substitute at best, since it meant driving Dad's sturdy but unexciting green Plymouth sedan. One of our friends, whose father was a surgeon, took his turns driving us around town in a large, blue Cadillac with huge tail fins that made it look more like a boat than a car. We didn't mind at all, as we cruised down the streets to numerous catcalls.

Cars were also a convenient place to become intoxicated. The drug of choice was alcohol and particularly beer. We heard of heroin addicts in big cities, but the chance of becoming hooked on anything like that terrified even the bravest. So, we stuck pretty much to the 3.2% by volume beer that we could buy in our state at age 18. Even when underaged, it was never hard to find an older brother or friend who would buy us a six-pack or two. If none of them were around, some store clerks would look the other way. Sometimes we even managed to buy a whole case of beer and took it out to some deserted place in the country. A favorite spot for illegal imbibing was a fire tower down in the hills. We seldom polished off a whole case of beer in one night and faced the problem of where to keep the leftovers. The family car was out of the question, forcing us to innovate. Once we stashed it in a small creek, which kept it cool until we could get back. Another time we broke into a church camp on a winter's night and hid it there.

Some of us did get a little tipsy on this low-powered beer, but we all hated the bitter taste at first. Even if we didn't get drunk, we pretended we were plastered and hoped the act was good enough to fool our friends who were behaving just as badly. To us, drinking beer illegally and pretending to be drunk was another sign of manhood. If most of us were still virgins, we at least could try to act like men by trying to drink like men. That it was both against the law and dangerous to life and limb made it even more attractive as a vehicle of teenage rebellion. We were lucky not to be badly hurt or killed in the process.

Music has also played an important part in the adolescent experience since at least the 1920s, and our generation was no exception. When we look back on the music of our time, we think of rock and roll stars like

Elvis Presley, Buddy Holly, and the Big Bopper. However, until the middle of the 1950s, the big band sound was very much alive, and the singers who dominated the charts were performers like Vaughn Monroe, Rosemary Clooney, or Perry Como. It was the sort of music our parents had liked during the war and that we have always associated it with their young adulthood. Finally, rock and roll gave us new musical references that we could own, especially since our parents hated it.

Rock and roll gave us a way to break with the lock-step precision demanded by the school, our coaches, our parents, and the church. The moment when this musical rebellion first hit our high school resulted from a mistake by the principal who invited back an old alum and successful jazz musician to play at a student assembly. Although the concert was intended to honor a former graduate and inspire us to go out and achieve something for ourselves, the jazz band "set fire" to the whole balcony filled with freshmen. It was jazz and not rock and roll, but there was something about its raucous sound that turned the freshmen into a stamping, clapping, bobbing horde. For teachers accustomed to the most docile behavior during assemblies, the whole performance was a frightening spectacle. It was music that gave us permission to dance rather than to march obediently.

Most of the singers and garage bands that we went on to admire and imitate are forgotten, in part because we considered the songs more important than the performers. Just as obsolete are the 45-single recordings they made, victims first to the long-playing records and then to tapes,

CDs, and later to the internet and various streaming platforms. Although the early rock and roll lyrics seem banal decades later, it was the new sounds and the hand-wringing adult disapproval that mattered most to us teenagers.

That such a raw and novel sound arose in the era of Ike, *The Ed Sullivan Show*, and crew haircuts, and that it provoked so much anxiety from adults, is surprising until we view it against a backdrop of widespread anxiety. The parents of our generation worried that such "undisciplined" music would lead to sloppy dress, bad manners, and even sexual immorality. One elderly neighbor complained, with more than a hint of racism, that we looked like a bunch of African savages dancing around the jungle floor. The fact that most of us kept wearing our letter sweaters and continued to go to the barber shop every two weeks for a good close cut did nothing to calm them down. All it took was one story of how Alice McKinley's son, once headed for the ministry, had instead grown ducktails and was believed to be a drinker, to confirm our parents' worst fears and convince them that they had to keep a tight lid on us. Some of the more hysterical adults, thankfully not including our parents, even wondered if the new music were some sort of insidious Communist plot.

At the time, we lived as if rock and roll music and mild adolescent rebellion would go on forever. In fact, there was no one moment, no crisp rite of passage, which separated our adolescence from early adulthood. The nearest thing to it was leaving town for college. One of us eventually became a history professor and the other a Presbyterian minister. Although we could not know it at the time, the Kennedy assassination in November 1963 would begin a decade of turmoil and violence that ended with the country's defeat in Vietnam and the forced resignation of Richard Nixon.

As we look back, we can find many faults with a town like ours: the cultural smugness, the racial inequality, the gender prejudices, and the exaggerated fears of Communism. At the same time, we are thankful for the safe and predictable rhythms of small-town life, at least for us, and for the baseline that it offered for understanding and appreciating the changes that would confront us in the years ahead.

DAVID CONTOSTA left the hometown to teach American history at several colleges and universities in the Philadelphia area. He is the author of more than 20 books. These publications include several regional topics, including  *Metropolitan Paradise: Philadelphia's Wissahickon Valley* and *Frontier Town to Edge City: Lancaster, Ohio, 1800-2000*, both of which have been adapted as documentary films. Other books focus on national and international themes: *Rebel Giants: The Revolutionary Lives of Abraham Lincoln and Charles Darwin* and *America's Needless Wars*. Additional titles include *The Private Life of James Bond* and *Henry Adams and the American Experiment*. At present he is writing a book about the American presidency. Contosta frequently gives walking tours through local neighborhoods, delivers talks to community groups, and is intensely interested in social and cultural history. He has lectured at Nanjing University in China and at Pyeongtaek University in South Korea and has been a Visiting Researcher at Cambridge University in England, as well as a Fulbright Scholar to France. Contosta lives at what was once a crossroads village near Philadelphia.

PHILIP HAZELTON left home to attend theological seminary and was ordained as a Presbyterian minister. During his career, he served churches in suburban Baltimore, Maryland; Bluffton, Indiana; suburban Detroit; and Worthington, Ohio. His church work and  personal cares extended to numerous community activities, including the promotion of mental health services, city parks, youth sports, and Head Start, and he was the founder of the Rev. Dr. Philip Hazelton AIDS/HIV Center in South Africa. Hazelton also published two books, *The High Places*, a collection of 13 sermons, and *Tuesday Faces*, containing weekly stories about biblical characters. He had mastered the artistic technique of pointillism, made famous by the late nineteenth-century painter Georges Seurat, and skillfully used this medium to illustrate each of his 52 biblical characters. He was also an amazing storyteller, as evident in this memoir of childhood and in his preaching, which enthralled members of his congregations and grew church memberships wherever he served. Philip and his wife Judy were living in suburban Columbus at the time of his death several years ago.

JULIA OLSZEWSKI is pursuing a degree in art history and curatorial studies at Temple University's Tyler School of Art. Julia brings to this work a fresh and ever-growing worldview supplemented by their life-long affinity for art. Julia has taken multiple courses in Islamic art history, Afro-Caribbean art and Regional West African practices. They are currently centering their focus on consciousness as it applies to art practice across various genres. They have applied consciousness studies to religious theory as well, producing a paper entitled *Lespri: Representation of the Haitian Mind Through Vodou Art and Practice.* As Julia develops more knowledge in Arts administration, they intend to apply it towards a career in management of exhibit spaces. They have written multiple academic papers regarding acquisition of global artifacts by colonizing western institutions and the implications of a restorative and reimagined community museum structure. Uniting all these rivulets of interest and research, Julia is looking at the future of an unbound museum, no longer restricted by the white cube mindset and liberated by the sharing of all human creation.

CPSIA information can be obtained
at www.ICGtesting.com
Printed in the USA
LVHW090808050422
715267LV00018B/2394